MORE THAN 1000 YEARS OF MARCH

TREVOR BEVIS

CHAPTER CONTENTS

ILLUSTRATED BY THE AUTHOR

WESTRYDALE PRESS

Copyright - T. BEVIS 1984 - ISBN 0 901680 23 0

ARCHITECTURAL HERITAGE YEAR

Published by T. Bevis, 150 Burrowmoor Road, March, Cambs PE15 9SS
Tel: 0354 57286

Printed by Cambs. Printcentre Ltd., 30 Coningsby Road, Peterborough
PE3 8SB   Tel: 0733 265246

Frontispiece: Attractive 19th century Cottages, Nene Parade, March

INTRODUCTION...

HENRY Ford of America once said "History is bunk." He was good but how much better he would have been if he had understood the past. History spotlights pitfalls, thereby providing a visual foundation for the present. The fortunes and misfortunes of the past, prescribed in full circles give a studied glimpse into the future.

The history of March is a story of struggle in an environment entirely dominated by nature — sweet one moment and sour the next. The will to survive against plague and to conserve what was the Fenman's right... the right to fish and to take fowl, to reap and sow, to gather reeds and breed fine horses. This was opposed by men visualising more prolific undertakings. In getting their way the drainage undertakers heaped redundancy and misery upon the Fenmen but their descendants reaped bountiful harvests.

From rags to riches is true of many Fenmen. From riches to rags is equally true, the Fen often turning upon men and ruining them. March has had its ups and downs. It never seemed to work towards a future but always fell upon its feet. Its past was never gilt edged but it has a social history of profound educational value and goes one better than most places in possessing the memory of its very own saint. Many places are traceable to the Norman Conquest — but on the strength of its saint March can be credited with at least 300 years before that event.

Fact is entwined with assumption. Hereward must have known Merc during his dreary existence alluding the Normans in the "Wide Sea" nearby. Oliver Cromwell surely knew March as he passed through the Fens on his way to Wisbech and Needham Hall. Certainty can be credited to the adroitness of various scribes. A wealth of information has passed down to historians in the form of churchwardens books, documents and registers. The monks of Ely were not idle either, diligently recording the holdings of March and other parishes and of the men and women that worked them. March scribes listened to the parish meeting in the south porch of the church and recorded all, witnessed by the lions of March carved upon the entrance of the porch.

❧ This book can only portray a glimpse of the town's past, some items re-written from the author's previously published parts with additional information, to which is added several new illustrations relevant to the past and present. It is hoped this offering will portray the town's past to some extent at least in an interesting and evocative manner, and in part make up for a dearth of published knowledge about our historic, if modest, Fen town.

Trevor Bevis.

March, Cambridgeshire.

The Lions of March
St. Wendreda's Church

Cruisers moored on the river at March

CHAPTER I

The Beginning

T is certain that March began as a settlement in the Saxon era. The close proximity of a couple of Romano–British encampments about a mile north of the River Nene – on rising ground at Grandford and a short distance east, at Flaggrass Hill, along the line of a Roman causeway stretching from near Denver in Norfolk to Fengate, Peterborough – sited on existing March boundaries in no way indicate that the town was established during Roman times. That the Romans frequented the area is indisputable. Even before they came to Britain the Beaker folk left a sample of their ware near the town site. Apart from sites already mentioned artifacts from the Roman period were discovered in Robingoodfellows Lane and one or two other sites in March. At Stonea nearby it seems that a temple had been built. These sites occupied relatively dry land and the slight prominences or hills became islands when the area surrounding them was inundated sometime after the Romans left the country in about 400 A.D. By 600 A.D. the area, according to Wulphere formed an impassable swamp and there were extensive meres. Islands were the habitations of recluse people inspired by the grand isolation – a suitable environment for religious devotion and enlightenment in spiritual and natural things. Many of these individuals were later canonised and monasteries erected in their honour. The monasteries were savagely attacked by the Danes and islanders put to fire and sword. From the ruins rose new walls and plain chant heard again from the islands confirmed that the Fens were the Holy Land of the English.

The settlement of Merch or Merc occupied the north end of a Fen island – the second largest – at nearly 30 feet above sea level. It would be bold indeed to pre-date March before 650 A.D. but it is reasonable to underline the years between 650 and 675 as the period of the town's foundation. This can be based on the coming of Wendreda, by all accounts a lady possessing healing powers. It is possible she found a few people living there and that the good woman desired to help them in their malarial existence. On the other hand if she had the same inclinations of Paega, a Christian recluse and sister to Guthlac of Crowland, who established a cell on the little Fen island of Peakirk (Paega's church) in the early eighth century, Wendreda too may have desired a life of solitude on a lonely island surrounded by marsh.

Logical conclusions do not support that possibility as we are dealing with a saint who had already enjoyed helping people in accordance with her calling as a missionary and healer. She is said to have had an understanding with animals too and that they too sought her help. It would not therefore seem justifiable for her to abandon her good work in favour of an uninhabited island. Perhaps she nurtured the desire to work towards her final days from a church of her own foundation, as did others, with a few handmaidens administering to the needs of a few fisher-folk, but more important as Wendreda was concerned, to introduce or enlarge the Christian faith to this part of the Fens.

It is proper to refer to her as Saint Wendreda of Exning and March. The first mentioned Suffolk village witnessed the development of her abilities and Merc witnessed her demise. Also known as St. Mindred and St. Mildred, Wendreda tends to be outshone by King Anna's saintly daughters, Etheldreda, Sexburga, Ethelburga, Sethrid and Withburga, all of whom were canonised. They were all familiar with Exning where their father had a large palace. It has been suggested that Wendreda was another daughter of the godly King whose home was deserted after his and his son's death in battle against the Danes and his wife retired to a nunnery in France. Almost certainly the Royal household knew of Wendreda, and they being Christians loved and respected her.

Long ago there was a holy well at Exning fed by springs containing unusual healing properties. It is thought that the great missionary Felix baptised King Anna and his family at this well which was named after St. Wendreda. The King's daughters were destined to establish great ecclesiastical foundations but Wendreda has no such prime monument dedicated to her, save for the lovely mediaeval church at March.

We might visualise Wendreda as a woman of retiring nature, devoted to her faith and dedicating her gifts totally for the health and benefit of the afflicted. As a child she may well have played with the princesses in the meadows at Exning. The springs bearing her name have been desicrated by a bypass and there is no longer peace in that place. Much of Wendreda's life was spent there and through her compassion and wisdom arose the virtues necessary for one destined for sainthood. There in the meadows she received the halt and lame, the sick and dying and comforted them with the waters from her holy well. An excellent listener and counsellor as indeed she had to be, Wendreda's fame spread far and wide and Exning became a name of hope. When King Anna had died and his daughters had gone their separate ways Exning began to decline. This became complete with the establishment of Newmarket in the 13th century.

The western area of the Fens were mainly converted by monks of Celtic origin. They were different to the missionaries from Europe. Celtic monks formed a number of monasteries of independent and quite different rules to monks belonging to Roman orders. Monks with total allegience to Rome introduced Christianity to the East and Mid Fen districts. Wendreda obviously knew of the malarial fens and the larger islands upon which wretchedly poor inhabitants struggled to survive and possibly practised heathen rituals. The people stiffened from the perpetually damp environment and the ague took heavy toll of them. They were probably too involved with survival to notice the matchless dawns and sunsets, a quality appreciated and understood by recluse individuals who were busy setting up their cells on the islands.

Thus Wendreda came to Merc more than thirteen centuries ago. The island was approximately six miles long and two miles wide and contained woodland and marsh. Inhabitants lived a hum-drum life and they and their offspring suffered a high mortality rate. Their main diet comprised mainly of fish and eels and wildfowl which were plentiful. Dwellings were made of framework daubed with clay and dung and reeds were used for thatch. There was a sense of security derived from the protective marsh and meres and rivers merging in the winter formed natural moats against undesirable visitors. No-one knows how long Wendreda lived on this island but there can be no doubt that her presence there was beneficial to all.

One of Wendreda's first priorities was to erect a building for use as a church. It was the forerunner to the existing ancient church. If she was accompanied by other women then more buildings were required – thus establishing the long tradition of March having had a nunnery. Reeds covered the floors and skins covered the openings in the walls. Vermin thrived in these places. With the coming of Wendreda to March (Merc means "boundary") the settlement must have been a Mecca to Fen folk. To have a healer and counsellor in their midst would not go unobserved and she was undoubtedly known to the inhabitants of the higher ground encircling the Fens. It would be surprising if many strangers had not gone to Merc in the summer. Her Exning achievements surely preceded her to Merc. She did not go to the settlement to start all over again but rather to end her days in service to God and men sharing with them their wretched environment. Other holy people preferred to begin their ministries in the Fens. One feels that Wendreda preferred to live with ordinary people and she chose this last post the conditions of which was seen by her as a challenge to her faith, fortitude and humility.

Wendreda was buried at Merc in a coffin covered with precious and semi precious gems and lapis lazuli. For a time her remains rested on the island amidst the marshes and meres. There is no known record of St. Wendreda's canonisation. The first thousand years of English Christianity produced numerous saints. Truly godly people were canonised by procedures barely recognisable in our own time. It was a relatively simple matter to create saints. Wherever the Christian message was received the procedures of canonisation were jointly witnessed by congregations of bishops and laity. In a matter of weeks, depending upon evidence and proof the deceased person was declared a saint. It is thought the canonisation of St. Wendreda took place between 700 and 800 A.D.

Nowadays canonisation is a highly involved business necessitating considerable investigation headed by lawyers and others of the highest intellectual status. These procedures can last many, many years. Needless to say it was partly through the army of saints that monasteries became very complex and powerful and fabulously wealthy. The religious foundation at Ely was in a flourishing condition and Abbot

Aelsi with a mind to increasing the wealth of his estate began to accumulate relics and enshrine them at Ely. It made sense to him that the relic of St. Wendreda be numbered with her sister saints from the Royal House of Anna. King Ethelred the Second, favourably disposed towards Aelsi, gave to the monks of Ely the village of Littlebury (Lib. Elien M.S.) and endorsed the abbot's desire "to translate the holy virgin Saint Wendreda from the village of Merch to Ely which he (the abbot) enclosed in a shrine of gold adorned with precious stones"(Ibid. cap. 76, 77). We will learn in a later chapter more about St. Wendreda and the effect she had upon Merch and Mercheford

When a notable religious recluse had died and had received canonisation it was usual for a monastery – or even a small church – to be built on the site of his or her cell. This procedure followed in the case of St. Pega (Peakirk), St. Guthlac (Crowland), Sts. Tancred, Tortred and Tona (Thorney), St. Huna (Chatteris), St. Felix (Soham), St. Etheldreda (Ely) and her sisters St. Sexburga (Isle of Sheppey), and St. Withburga (East Dereham). It would have been very unusual for March and St. Wendreda to be the exception to the rule. That nuns lived at March and continued in the footsteps of St. Wendreda was highly likely although no written evidence of a pre-Conquest nunnery ever having existed at March has yet come to light. The discovery of large blocks of stone near ancient stew ponds in the vicinity of St. Wendreda's church does seem to indicate that a post-Conquest building of large proportions once existed at March. That an ecclesiastical building existed at March before the Norman Conquest is perfectly feasible. The recorded fact that St. Wendreda was buried – even enshrined here – and had clearly entered sainthood while her remains lay at March must stress the point that a church of some importance stood here and welcomed pilgrims probably to the very same site or very near the existing mediaeval church. There is some record that nuns lived at March over several centuries.

CHAPTER II

1066 and all that

PRE-CONQUEST Merc comprised of a scattering of crude dwellings. There were not many residents, far less than at
Dodintona which until as recently as the 19th century
held a higher status than did March. Townships attach great
importance to William the Conqueror's famous national
survey - Domesday - compiled in 1086. March is included
in the Manor of Doddington in survey form undertaken before the much
quoted Norman assessment. It agrees with the Domesday version and
includes a number of additions under the title of "Ely Inquest":

"The Abbot of Ely used to hold Dodintona in the time of King
Edward and renders an account of 5 hides and at the present cultivates
8 ploughlands. There is land for 3 ploughs and in the demense farms
are 2½ hides. There are 500 men on the Manor. 24 villein tenants
have each of them 7½ acres. There are 8 cottager tenants. 8 sochemen
have one hide and there is a slave (with land). There are 8 carucates
of meadow and pasture for the stock of the inhabitants. There is
wood sufficient to feed 250 pigs. As to the fisheries, 27,150 eels
are paid and 24 shillings. There are 126 unemployed beast, 26 sheep,
64 pigs, 3 nags and 24 brood mares. The whole value of the Manor is
put at £16; formerly £10 was received. In the time of King Edward £12.
This Manor now is and used to be in the time of King Edward in the
lordship of the Abbot of Ely. And in this there is a certain hamlet
called Mercha which is included in the above valuation. And in the
same hamlet the Abbot of St. Edmunds holds 16 acres of whom the Abbot
of Ely has 'soccage'."

The same reference to the "hamlet of Mercha" is made in the Domesday
book. Most towns and villages in the Fens existed at the time of
William's survey in 1086. Several preserve a few visual stones from
those far-off times, usually in the form of churches and less noticeable
are castles. As far as Norman influence is concerned at March, a single
question arises: did the ecclesiastical powers that had replaced the
Saxon hierarchy at Ely order that a substantial church be erected at
March in place of any Saxon structure? It is a fact that the Normans
regarded Saxon architecture in an amusing light. Certainly they were
not slow to encourage the demolishment of the majority of Saxon churches
and build their own solid type of churches. Whereas the Saxons built
an edifice with economy in mind, the Normans built theirs to impart
strength and dominance to all that beheld them. Several Fen churches
possess Norman pillars and walls to which other ages added architectural additions. At March as far as we can tell no part of St.
Wendreda's church can be attributed to the Norman age, but the survival
of the font with its crude geometrical carvings testifies to the Norman

The main road was that of Knight's End skirting Lynwood. The commons
were sectioned by tracks and the present modern highway was one. Nearby
was a large expanse of arable land called Cunewood or Coneywood Field
which consisted of 100 acres let to 40 tenants. It was farmed in strips.
Near the south end of the island lay a prolific fishery, Dudingthnefrith:
In summertime it formed small pools but during winter it turned itself
into an extensive lake on which boats plied between Chatteris and Dod-
ington carrying supplies and messengers from Ely to Doddington Palace.

Slightly north east of Mercheford the areas of Elin and Derefield
succoured several orchards intersected by dykes. Mercheford was dis-
tinguished by its several messuages stretching on north bank accessible
by means of a track later called Whittle-End (at present West End), and
Outer-End, later Well-End (at present Nene-Parade). The majority of the
hutments were occupied by freemen and tenant farmers. Fishermen lived
there too working on the river and the meres. From near the ford buildings flanked a rough track leading to Northwood Common (Norwood Side).
It later developed into Bridge Street (Broad Street) and continues in
the existing Robingoodfellows Lane. Mercheford is mentioned in Bishop
John de Fordham's register (1394) concerning conveyance of property to
John de Mercheford of London. John was a native of Mercheford but he
left the Fens to work at London. He apparently did well for himself
and purchased property in his native town totalling an acre "lying
between the messuage of Thomas Stevenson and the common drain (river)
on the other side". There were 97 dwellings at Mercheford in 1287,
hutments made up of 81 messuages, 10 half messuages, one one-third of a
messuage and five quarter messuages. These were strips of land farmed
by tenants living on the respective sites. Ecclesiastical records name
77 tenants for that year with holdings and rent:

MERCHEFORD TENANTS, HOLDINGS AND RENT FOR YEAR 1287

Richard, son of Ralph
2 holdings 1s.
(over the water)
Godlam, son of Aylmer
1, 6d.
Thomas of Walsoken
1 & a bit, 7d.
Henry Champneis
2 & 2 bits, 1s. 2d.
Ralph Dowe 1, 6d.
Richard of Wesbaye
1 & a bit, 7d.
Robert of Hydele &
Geoffrey Nossy 1, 4d.
Deke Gaze $\frac{1}{2}$, 3d.
Richard, son of
Thomas 1 & 1 third,
8d.

John of Benuik 1, 6d.
Henry, son of Elena
1, 6d.
Aldus Tholy 1 & a bit,
7d.
Richard, son of Hugh
1 & a bit, 7d.
Richard his brother
1 & a bit, 7d.
Eva Turgeis 2, 1s.
Robert Schod 1 & a bit,
7d.
Christina Muck &
Richard the Coverer
1, 6d.
Philip Clerk 1, 6d.
David Spendlove 1, 6d.

Robert of Esteworch
Henry, son of Walter
1, 6.
John Bull 1 & a bit 7d.
Stephen of Strahan
1 & a bit, 7d.
Reginald Clerk 1, 6d.
Henry, son of Elena
1, 6d.
David Spendlove
$\frac{1}{4}$, 1$\frac{1}{2}$d.
Amicia, daughter of
David 1, 6d.
William Tincerna 1, 6d.
Peter, son of Thomas
1, 6d.
Ralph, son of Richard
$\frac{1}{2}$ & a bit, 4d.

- 8 -

Walter Palmer, John of Benuick, John son of Hugh 1 bit, ½d.
Everard Gaze 1, 6d.
Henry Tympson 1, 6d.
Richard Sperhard 2, 1s.
Walter Seul (½ mess. and a bit, 5d.
Peter Chapman 1½, 9d.
Thomas son of Roger Abbott ¼, 2d.
Richard Sperhard ¼, 2d.
Richard Abbott ½, 3d.
John Shepherd 1, 6d.
Wymark Sepayn 2, 1s.
Walter Mumby 1, 6d.
Agnes Oppere 1, 6d.
Henry Sepayn 1, 6d.
Ralph son of Godfrey 1 & a bit, 7d.
Walter the Palmer 2, 1s.
Richard son of Hugh 1, 6d.

Alicia, widow of Gilbert; John son of Hugh 1, 6d.
Richard Clayhand 2, 1s.
Geoffrey Pecok 1, 6d.
Clement the son of John 1, 6d.
Ralph son of William 3, 1s. 8d.
Richard son of Odo 1, 1½ acres marsh, 9d.
Reginald Clerk ¼, 2d.
Richard of Wynebolesham ¼, 1½d.
Eliote Hunte 2, 1s.
Stephen of Strathan 1, 6d.
John Cugeray 1, 6d.
Eliot son of Joly 1 & a bit, 6d.
Henry Champneis 1, 6d.
Henry son of Thomas 2, 2s.
Reginald and Robert of Hydele 2, 1s.

Stephen Gaze 1, 6d.
David Spendlove 1, 6d.
Ralph son of Godfrey 2, 1s.
Agnes, daughter of Joly 1, 6d.
Peter son of Thomas (½, 4d.)
Robert of Esteworch 1, 6d.
Robert Schad 1, 6d.

Matthew Shepherd 1, 6d.
Roger Cut 1, 6d.
Robert son of Richard 1 & a bit, 7d.
Richard Gaze 1½, 8d.
John Em 2 half mess. 6d.
Gilbert the Coverer 1, 6d.

The cottars (cottagers) at Merche and Mercheford were obliged to carry out duties in labour rent to the lord of the manor. In addition to such obligatory duties the cottar had also to attend on his own account the hired land listed with the above names. The great boon day (gratis work day) was accepted with dubious toleration. Each able bodied cottar had to perform extra tasks as part rent for the lord at Doddington which necessitated a four or five mile walk or ride from the settlements. The cottars were given loaves and flesh and fish, cheese and beer and then allocated tasks at various places which fell within the manor boundaries, such as "Strode in Doddington and carry timber for inclosure and rods to Dereford (Merche) and there make or repair a cow-house and a calves' cote when need is at their own proper cost with the lord's timber, but the lord shall find the master carpenter and they shall daub the said houses (with clay) and close the walls and roof, and cut, bind and carry the reed for same. They are obliged to mow the lord's manor at Dereford, to make the hay and stack it and they have two cheeses of the better sort, and two lots of buttermilk found in the churn - that is as much as is collected in one week. He must carry goods with his neighbour on long and short journeys. Short to Rosby at Elm, Myrmaunde Priory at Upwell, and Coldham, if need be without refreshment. Long to Wysebeche and Wellbreche, the lord providing the food. The cottars and all customary tenants at Merche ought to carry one cargo of cheese from Mercheford to Lynn . . . once in the year".

A winding track, Lionell's Causeway, partly survives in the existing Wisbech Low Road; it passed over the Chain area and linked Mercheford with Elm and Wisbech. According to Bishop Alcock's register in 1487 it was renamed Southewolde's Causeway presumably to honour an influential local family. The road was hazardous, especially during winter and passed through thick woodland skirting dangerous marsh. Adjacent land was "common" and Northwood to the west harboured herds of swine and thieves. Hereabouts John Fuller and his wife, Amy, formerly of Haddenham, while passing along the Causeway were set upon by robbers. They lost their horse and 15s. together with a hundred ells of cloth.

The Bishop of Ely deemed Northwood a favourable area and he had a dairy farm there. Who would dare to steal from him! The Bishop had similar farms at Westry, Dereford (Dartford) and Esteworch (Estover). A neighbour, Simon the Chamberlain, also farmed at Esteworch and he worked in addition 120 acres of Marsh. Simon was a Freeman but many of his friends were little more than slaves. A document written in 1257 states that Dereford contained $15\frac{3}{4}$ acres of well watered land and $45\frac{3}{4}$ acres of meadow. It fed 40 cows and a couple of free bulls. Plenty of hay was obtainable, and "be it known that the whole township of Merche ought to mow and make the hay and carry it from $22\frac{1}{2}$ acres, including Hethwood, Sidehale, Shetain, Westrydale, Newesdale, Ledeole, Elrenho and near Hithedol. Fine old March names. Estwode (Eastwood) provided 19 acres of meadow.

Several people with titles lived in Merche and Mercheford, no less than 25 as knights and free tenants. They farmed a total of 573 acres. Stephen de Marisco (of the marsh) held 40 acres for 6s. 8d., this situated in Hatchwood. Thomas Aulton held three carucates (that is as much land as a plough can cultivate) for 43s. per year. Simon of Esteworch managed the dairy farm rented at 5s. and the marsh cost him 6s. 8d. Osbert de Mountford held 30 acres of marsh in Mumfords — which lay in Creek area. Richard son of Thomas occupied 8 acres of arable land at 4s. per annum and 7 acres of marsh at 1s. 2d. Thomas Aulton believed in shrewd thinking. Highland on which he kept bullocks was safe from inundation and valued at over 43s. It was valuable. Here and there highland and marsh mingled and is better described as coarse fen, under water for six months of the year.

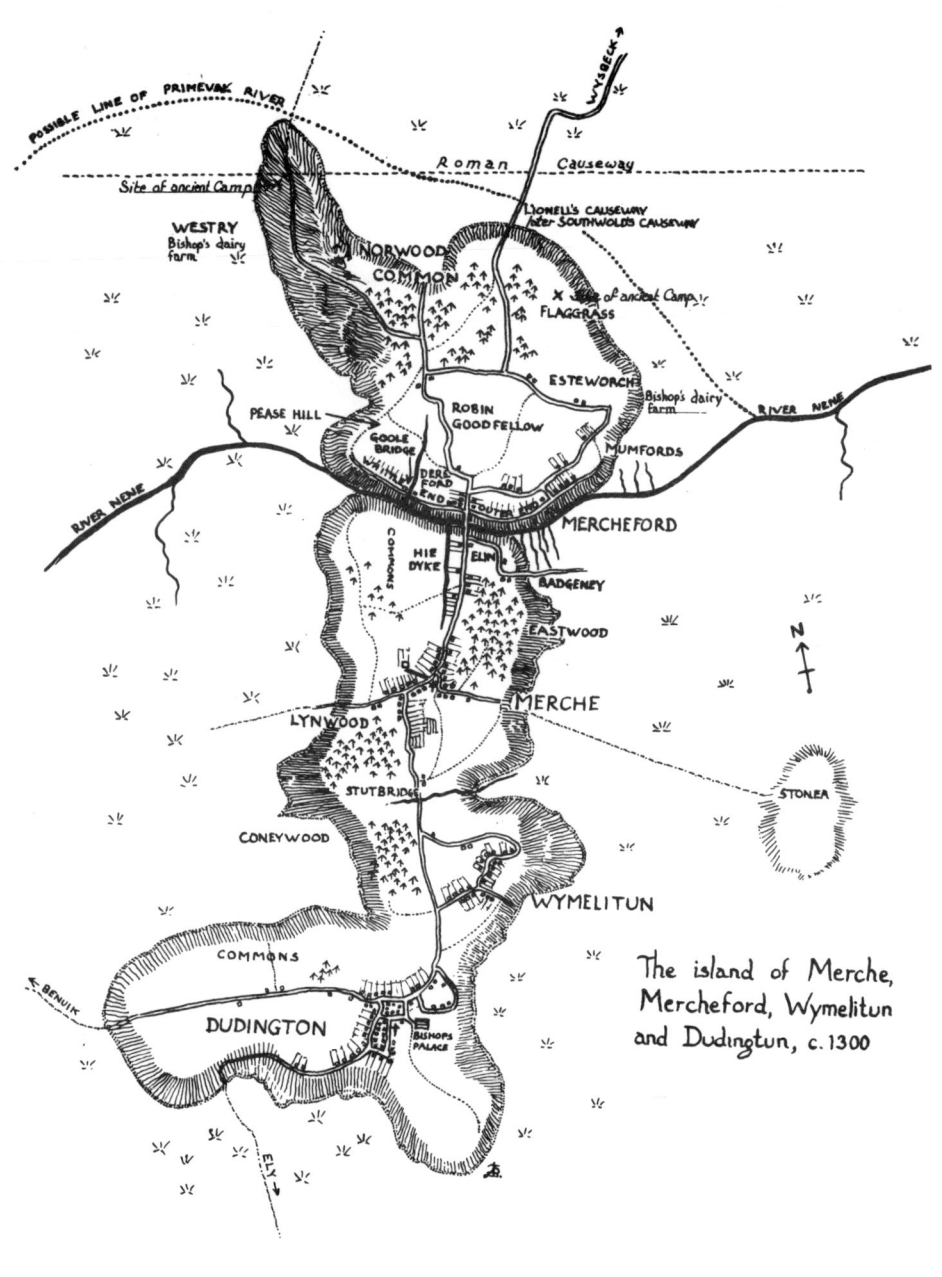

POSSIBLE LINE OF PRIMEVAL RIVER

Roman Causeway

Site of ancient Camp

WESTRY
Bishop's dairy farm

NORWOOD COMMON

LIONELL'S CAUSEWAY
later SOUTHWOLD'S CAUSEWAY

× Site of ancient Camp
FLAGGRASS

ESTEWORCH
Bishop's dairy farm

RIVER NENE

PEASE HILL

ROBIN GOODFELLOW

GOOLE BRIDGE

WHITTLE
DERE LOAD
SOUTH END
MUMFORDS

RIVER NENE

MERCHEFORD

HIE DYKE

ELM

COMMONS

BADGENEY

EASTWOOD

N

MERCHE

LYNWOOD

STUTBRIDGE

STONEA

CONEYWOOD

WYMELITUN

← BENWIK

COMMONS

DUDINGTON

BISHOPS PALACE

ELY ↓

The island of Merche,
Mercheford, Wymelitun
and Dudingtun, c.1300

WYSBECK ↑

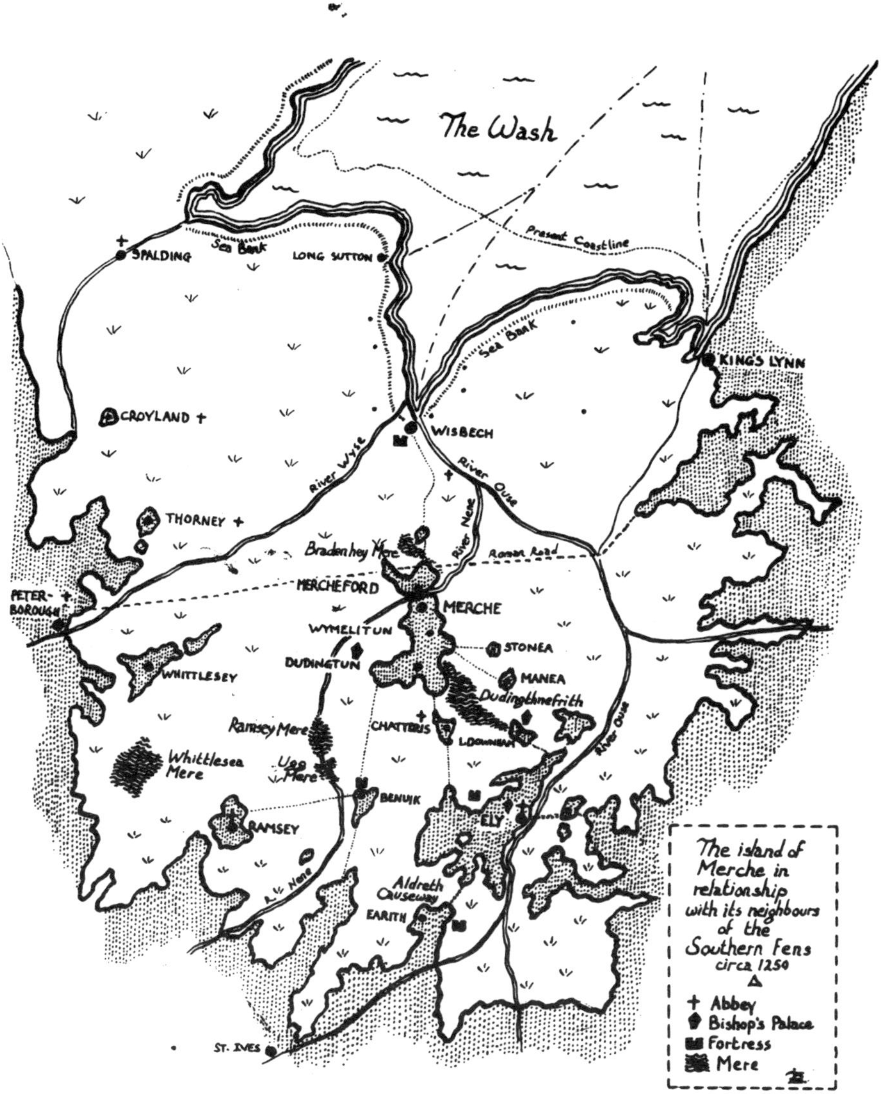
The Wash
Present Coastline
Sea Bank
SPALDING
LONG SUTTON
Sea Bank
KINGS LYNN
CROYLAND
WISBECH
River Wyse
River Ouse
River Nene
THORNEY
Bradenhey Mere
Roman Road
PETER-BOROUGH
MERCHEFORD
MERCHE
WYMELITUN
STONEA
DUDINGTUN
WHITTLESEY
MANEA
Dudingthnefrith
CHATTERIS
DOWNEAM
River Ouse
Ramsey Mere
Whittlesea Mere
Ugg Mere
BENUIK
ELY
RAMSEY
R. Nene
Aldreth Causeway
EARITH
ST. IVES
The island of Merche in relationship with its neighbours of the Southern Fens circa 1250
Abbey
Bishop's Palace
Fortress
Mere

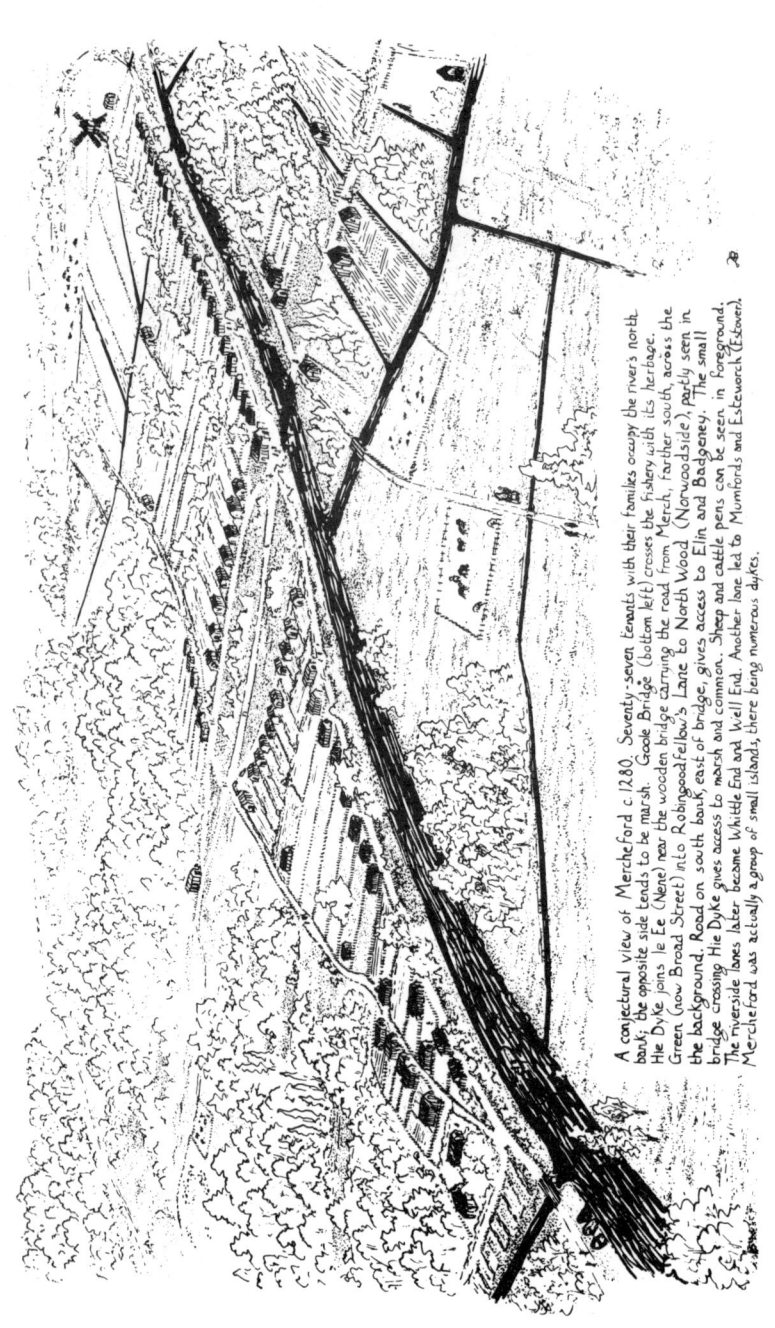

A conjectural view of Mercheford c.1280. Seventy-seven tenants with their families occupy the river's north bank; the opposite side tends to be marsh. Goole Bridge (bottom left) crosses the fishery with its herbage. Hie Dyke joins Ie Ee (Nene) near the wooden bridge carrying the road from Merch, farther south, across the Green (now Broad Street) into Robingoodfellow's Lane to North Wood (Norwoodside), partly seen in the background. Road on south bank, east of bridge, gives access to Elin and Badgeney. The small bridge crossing Hie Dyke gives access to marsh and common. Sheep and cattle pens can be seen in foreground. The riverside lanes later became Whittle End and Well End. Another lane led to Mumfords and Eskeworth (Eskover). Mercheford was actually a group of small islands, there being numerous dykes.

A conjectural drawing of March (Town End) about 1550. Right of the church spire can be seen the Guildhall (renamed 'Towne House'). To the left of the church stands the 'Treasure House' where town valuables were stored. The remains of a forest (Eastwood) is seen top left. The main road from Merchford passes the steeple to Wimblington via Lynwood and Millgate. Narrow strips of arable land are reminiscent of medieval 'strip' or corridor cultivation. Land in the foreground was known as Bell Fields. The churchyard is bounded on two sides by dwellings and shops. Eastwood manor stands off Barkers Lane, and Steeple Lane (opposite the tower) probably led to a nunnery, a stew pond existing until about 1960.

The oldest stone carving in March   AD 1100-1150.
FONT   ST. WENDREDA'S CHURCH

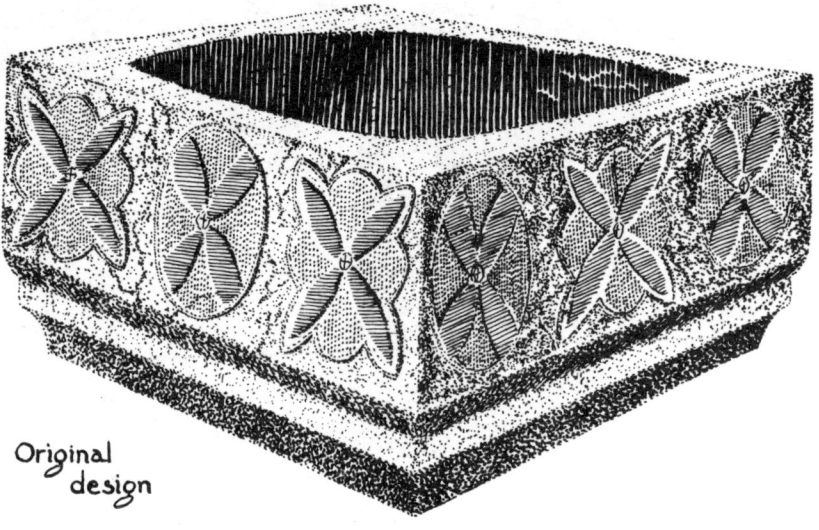

Original
design

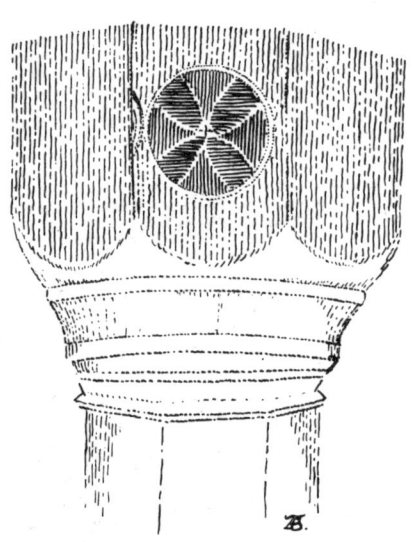

The corners of the Norman font have been erased to conform to the octagonal design of the church pillars. The basin, which retains a few crude geometrical designs was placed upon a medieval pedestal (left). The survival of this ancient font, despite mutilation, indicates the existence of a Norman church on this site prior to the general rebuilding in the 14th century.

CHAPTER III

Manorial Customs

USTOMARY tenants at Merche, Mercheford and Doddington worked hired lands in the heat of the day — from dawn until dusk. In winter they and their families huddled in skins for warmth on floors strewn with reeds and straw, the breeding ground of vermin. Smoke from open fires swirled everywhere before passing through a hole in the centre of the roof. There were problems enough and all too often families went short of food to the point of starvation. As late as the 13th century the struggle to abolish shackles forged by the feudal manorial system had begun. The system was vigorously practised by bishops and abbots holding as they did substantial land rights as well as barons who had inherited estates as reward for an ancestor's military prowess in service to the monarch. The process of elevation from the low status of serf to respected yeomen went forward in fits and starts spurred on by increasing knowledge and what was to be the new order of things. Norman influence was on the wane. The social life of the emergent English, speaking with a national tongue, directed the trend towards inventiveness in theroretic and practical lines. This blueprint is still proceeding.

Thus in the late 13th century the inhabitants of Merche and Mercheford stood at the threshold of great changes. There were instances where good and faithful tenants received just reward from their masters, a local example seen in the case of Bishop Hugh and Amisuis de Bennigden concerning 70 acres of land in Elm and Mercheford. Forty acres lay within the boundaries of the latter place and this with the remainder of the land was given to Amisuis and his heirs to have and hold in free service "for ever" at a rent of 2s.

Several disputes arose over the Manor lands and marshes at Merche, Dodintona and Wymelitun involving land and marsh which had interesting names. One such dispute heard at Dodintona in the reign of Richard II, concerned Bywere Moor (Burrowmoor), Brudenhee, Bulmerepool which lay close to the River Nene, a marsh called Beche, Hackepool and Wadesdrauht. Other areas within the dispute were Philippesdiche, Newi-Wysamouth and Ramsham (Ransonmoor). An ancient map by Moore clearly' displays a bank and the place Wig- or Wysamouth near the river at Copalder. Philippesdiche is not easily placed but it is supposed to be that area between Doddington and Benwick. The manuscript outlining the dispute mentions "lunaliter" — the curved or half moon shaped of the river between Copalder and March bridge. Another dispute mentioned in the Ely document refers to a "final peaceful settlement made in the Kings at Westminster in the reign of King Henry, the son of King John between Hugh, Bishop of Ely and Hugh, Bishop of St. Neots relating to

12 acres of marsh in ^Mercheford carrying animals, sheep feeding and
boats carrying burdens. There were numerous disputes between the
Bishop of Ely and Abbots of Ramsey and other places over land and marsh
rights.

Strip, or corridor cultivation was common throughout mediaeval
England. The customary tenants employed at March and Doddington in the
last half of the 13th century understood it well. ^Usually they worked
on an arable field of 100 acres, this divided into strips amounting to
several half acres and roods. The strips were measured as one rod wide
and 40 rods long, later known as furlong or furrowlong. Similar fields
of similar proportions were destined for winter wheat and the other
fallow. Men, women and children of the communities worked the land,
the latter usually leading oxen which dragged ploughs and bush harrows.

Many problems beset the customary tenant. Long winters threatened
his livestock and at harvest time he was obliged to watch the parsons
man walking in his strip along rows of sheafs, putting a little twig in
every tenth sheaf, that being reserved as tithe. In 1250 most March
tenants were classed "free", but the customary workers at Doddington
were low class with little or no capital. Through sheer hard work they
raised themselves from an even lower standard. Doddington workers found
it necessary to band together and form a virgate of land. What kind of
work did the Men of Merche carry out for the Bishop? On demand he had to
leave his own strip to enclose the lord's corn, to cut wood and carry it,
to provide a perch of hedge for each head of his stock; this hedge was
given to him when harvest had been completed.

In each week from Michaelmas to the Invention of the Cross (May 3)
he owed two days work to the Lord of the Manor, being Wednesday and
Friday excepting 15 days at Christmas and certain other days. The
customary worker had to plough 7 roods and harrow it in winter and at
Lent, finding his own food. He had to find a man to hoe for a whole day
and he received a loaf and two herrings. But for another similar day he
put his hoe to the ground without food. He mowed when necessary from
early in the morning until the ninth hour, in which time he stacked the
hay "without food". Much of the customary tenant's time was spent at
Stonea and for working there he was allowed a cow, an ox or heifer from
Stonea livestock.

Boonday brought its problems (it means a day's work given to the
lord as a present!). If the customary worker was ill he had to find a
man to fill his place. Men and women reaped the corn and each received
four loaves and soup with a dish of cheese and meat and beer. Their duty
was to gather, tie and shock the wheat on the day of reaping and if that
was not completed they had to return a second day. A man with his own
horse and cart carried three loads in all. Two men were responsible for
reaping reeds at Waterbedreppe and they, too, were found food. Workers
plied themselves on the lord's behalf nine hours a day, the remaining
daylight hours being utilised on their own strips. Numerous other tasks
were allocated to them, such as mowing, tying and preparation and trans-

portation to the manor house of 40 sheaves for brewing. The workers
used their own animals to cart the lord's several goods, on short
journies to Merche, Mercheford, Beenwick, Stoneye and Chateris, providing their own food; and in long journies to Ely, Dunham, Ditton,
Cambridge, Willingham, St. Ives, Somersham, Yaxley, Burgh St. Peter
(Peterborough), Wichleseye (Whittlesey), Thorney, Ramsey and various
other places mainly be waterways "without food, except the said carrying be done on a day of his working, and if it shall happen that there
is a delay beyond one day and one night for the affairs of the lord,
then he (the workman) shall have his food, or it shall be counted to
him for a day's work if it happen on a work day".

Every worker was expected to carry dung and spread it over an area
of not less than half an acre within the space of nine hours. If he
desired to sell an ox, a colt or foal he must obtain licence, and if any
tenant, his son or daughter wished to marry, a fine had to be paid to
the lord. When a man became ill and indisposed for 15 days after, he
was quit of all work during that period. He was obliged to honour boon
days in harvest. Neither did death free him of obligation, the lord
claiming the best beast. The widow remained "in home and land for 30
days after her man's death – free and quit of all service".

The desmesne land of Merche and Doddintona bore interesting names:
Southhythehove, Stanninghove, Hochove, Tenstychhove, Brethove, Hoo,
Fenegedeshove, Hursthove – combining a total of 246 acres under six
ploughs of eight oxen each. Meadowlands at Doddintona were Birsnoot
$10\frac{3}{4}$ acres, Northfen meadow 10 acres, and Hoo Fen 15 acres. In the
11th century the village had a fine covering of 250 acres of island
forest. The windmill was newly erected in 1250 and all customary tenants
had to patronise it. Arable land amounted to $331\frac{3}{4}$ acres, mowing grass
$105\frac{1}{2}$ acres, meadowland $35\frac{3}{4}$ acres, woodland 30 acres, the two ecclesiastical parks 140 acres. At Dereford (Merche) lay $15\frac{3}{4}$ acres of well
watered land, $45\frac{3}{4}$ acres of meadow where 40 cows and two bulls with
offspring fed. The dairy farm was let for £6 at the will of the lord.

When the documents were written, Merche and Doddintona had a large
acreage of woodland and unenclosed pastures as well as Lammas meadows,
there being extensive hay fields given over to livestock on Lammas Day,
August 1st. The open strip system continued well into the 17th century.
At March in 1615 a hemp field of half and acre lay at the rear of the
present almshouses in The Avenue. The field was previously made up of
separate grass fields which were brought together to form an arable
inclosure bounded by baulks.

The open field system was broken up by the instigation of Inclosure
Acts between 1750 and 1820, bringing about great changes in agricultural
and pastoral spheres. The strip system was never popular and even in
the 14th century farmers attempted to get their strips together and find
profitable use for the intervening baulk by ploughing it up and by
making a wide strip out of two.

CHAPTER IV

The Fisheries

S prolific as agriculture seemed to be in and around Merche, it barely matched the harvest obtained from the fisheries which surrounded the island. During the winter when life at Merche and Mercheford was less tolerable than usual and the causeway which linked the two communities became a quagmire, and marshes around the island were no longer obvious, being covered with muddy water it was difficult to define the edges of summer pools where abounded large quantities of fish and eels. Small raised areas of land between Mercheford and Benuick became islands of a few hundred yards in length and breadth. These were used as harbours and were reasonably safe places for livestock. These remote fen places were strangely named, for instance, Pollingscote, Puerslode, Kecalne were all part and parcel of the vast Echenemoor marsh. Sadlebowcote lay near a bend in the river (lunatler). The marsh at Sadlebow Mile rose slightly and the river pursued its course to Dedemill and Westfencote (now West Fen). Large stones discovered there may well indicate the former existence of a small church, not unusual as several tiny churches served Fen inhabitants until the Reformation. Utless marsh extended to West Fen Lake and nearby Patimere. Anyone travelling along the river passed the tiny islet of Waleby, on to Upstaventwisel and the rising ground known as Upstavencote (the "cotes" were harbours) which divided Wisbech from March Goosetree area. Nearby rose Stoney-hurst and Alreye washed by the waters of Levermere and lastly Echenhe. Fine sounding names and what places for fishermen!

Fen fisheries were numerous in the Saxon era and right through to the Middle Ages. Products from the fisheries were valued by people of the highlands and were a source of wealth, particularly to the several Fen monasteries. Fishing in winter time was not always as prolific as the summer when lots of little pools were formed as waters receded for the season, thereby denying fish and eels escape routes to adjacent meres. Stretreche was a fishery which lay within the boundaries of March and with other fisheries was the property of West Dereham and St. Neots priories. Larger fisheries centred on Doddington, the earliest of the Saxon era possessed by Brithnoth, first abbot of Ely who also acquired 60 acres of marsh adjoining, as well as a weir. The abbot let this for 1,000 eels annually. The monastery at Ely acquired about the same time Stonea and its marsh, let for 2,000 eels annually.

Fisheries near March included Stanwere, Hyrdelode, Strode, Est Fen, Dampnwege, Bradenhey, Newere and Byremere (Burrowmoor). Bradenhey fishery was let to several March tenants, one of whom "Benedict, the son of William, holds the 12th right . . . and gives a rent of 1,000

eels and 6s. 6d. in money". Geological changes caused problems. When a
mere had gradually filled with mud it reverted to grass and reed, serving as a "cote" or harbour for sheep or cattle. Often water courses
changed route altogether making their way in other directions, forming
new meres. It was a balanced process governed entirely by nature.
"In Merche, Deynes, son of Reginald; Richard, son of Aylmer; Gilbert,
son of William hold Fordmere and Suthernke for 13s., and on account of
the drying up of the fishery the Lord Bishop has given them as recom-
pense four acres of marsh at Upstaven, free of charge". Bradeney Mere
too dried out between 1278 and 1378. It formed a considerable and
valuable fishery but nature turned it into grazing ground for livestock.
Moor's map of 1667 shows Great Bradimoor well drained fen. All that
remained of the mere was a small expanse of water known as Glasselake.
A severe drought may have dried out the mere, bearing in mind that in
1353, the year of the Dear Summer, England was devastated by a famine
and dearth. It was not until 1365 that violent rain occurred.
A drought such as that could have seriously affected the Fens and by
the time substantial rain had drenched the region the geological pattern
had changed.

The town of March had a few fisheries well within the community.
A memorandum written in the 16th century states that March was made up
of five wards, the inhabitants of whom were actively involved in clear-
ing fish from the River Nene. Dams were thrown across the river and
sections between dragged with nets.

"Memorandum: These be the ordinances made by the consent of the
whole township of March. First the town being divided into five
wardships, the first wardship as Norwoodsyde shall begin and fysh
the weir the first night; the second night Weetel-end (West End);
the third night Owghtward-end (Nene-parade); the fourth night Hye
dyke (High Street); the fifth night Townsend, so consequently to go
till the second weir be made, and then the wardship that shall fysh
the end weir shall ye next night fysh the forward weir and so depart
till all the rest of the wardships have fyshed their turn. And
further it is ordained that no man shall lay any bownetts within
24 ft. of the other side of the river upon pain of forfeiting his
common (right of fishing) for a year and a day. Furthermore we
ordain that the sett in the old ea (river) shall always go with
Toubett weir, and further we ordain that no man shall let or give
his profit there, but if he or they like not to fysh the said
fyshing the other without delay or hindrance take the common profit
to themselves".

This system was later replaced by another, letting the fisheries in
periods of five years to March tenants. From 1552 - 1557 John Shepperd
hired the fishing rights (£4) and Roger Bussey hired the rights for £8
13s. 4d. Succeeding tenants were William Coward de Bageny, Roger
Bussey and William Coward de Lambe (of the Lambe Inn). They were to

"drag but twys". Another memorandum of 1582 states "that the selling of common water and weres with the two stamps in the old eae in Burramore ys letten th Thomas Barret and William Walsom for five years next ensuinge for the yearly rent of ix li (£9) by the yere, and they do keep it as it hath been kept usually, provided that the toune shall have the drawing thereof at any time once in the yere at their pleasure and deliver- the selling to the toune in as peaceable and quiet possession as they now enter thereon, and not to let any inhabitant of the toune to drive or lay bow netts in the said common water". John Walsham of Norwoodside, a fisherman, was tenant in 1657 for £8 13s. 4d. and 15 years later John Neale occupied the river fishery for £9 8s. "and he is to have for his paines the drawing of the said water to his use twice every year . . . and no man to lay any bownetts, grigs, hives, or to use any gleavinge within the pools of the seyd sett".

By 1600 the value of March fisheries had considerably declined and in 1659 were worth only £1 6s. 8d. Part of the gradual decline can be attributed to the Reformation. Before the break with Rome meat was never eaten on Wednesdays and Fridays throughout Lent and many of the faithful kept it up throughout the year. Consequently fish were in great demand. A Mr. Verney of March for some reason could not eat fish at the best of times. He obtained a special dispensation from the Archbishop enabling him to eat meat during Lent.

The important Nene fishery was supplemented by that at Goole Bridge and Lantern Bridge, two lesser fisheries, the former near the corn mill on Norwoodside Common and the latter at Lanthorn Close near where now is sited March railway station. Goole Bridge fishery was part of a stream feeding into the River Nene, and with its herbage actually increased its value. It was let every five years. Robert Peerson in 1552 paid 1s. per quarter to fish there. The fisheries were dealt a resounding blow with the advent of the Drainage Scheme introduced by "interfering foreigners" whom the Fenmen could not bear the sight of. About 1650 the old Hobb Drain — the present Twenty Foot river — was widened together with several other existing rivers. The Fenmen did everything they could to hinder work and Mr. Moore, the surveyor, who was conveyed on his boat by four Dutch prisoners of war, doubtlessly kept a wary eye cast on the banks for signs of treachery! The fen people's livelihood was undoubtedly seriously affected by the drainage operations carried out by hundreds of Scottish and Dutch prisoners and Huguenot and Walloon workers, skilled in the art of embanking.

CONDITIONS FOR WORKING GOOLE BRIDGE FISHERY

1597 – Item the sett of Goale Bridge from Robert Neales yard end with the swathe (hay) of the droves on both sydes till our Lady Day at Sturbridge fayer (Cambridge) is letten to Robert Neale – (Rent 11s.).

1637 – The Gole Bridge with the pingle to Thomas Coolidge for 29s., provided that if it be damaged by the undertakers (drainage workers) the town shall make him satisfaction.

THE NENE BRIDGES.

Long ago the River Nene was much higher than now and fordable. Successive excavations to lower the river to the level of the surrounding fen had the effect of confining it between unusually high banks. The result is not unattractive, in fact, the river aspect is one of great beauty, un-Fenlike even, and clearly an asset to the town. No longer a commercial highway, the river carries increasing numbers of pleasure craft served a short distance to the west by a small marina. The tourist season introduces an appreciable number of cruisers and long boats and a not insignificant collection of "home" craft are frequently berthed alongside owners private riverside gardens sheltered by fine trees. The ancient ford occupied the present site of the bridge and it is likely that the river was sufficiently high for that purpose until the 15th century when it is believed that a wooden bridge was erected. The earliest mention of a bridge occurs in an account of 1544 and a toll was charged to cross it. In 1557 Robert Pett had charge of the toll and he received payment of 7s. at Lammas time (August 1st). Roger Boze and Thomas Gibbs undertook this responsibility in 1570 (8s. per annum) and we learn that in 1576 John Brod acted as toll keeper at a rental of 15s. A shop stood at one end of the bridge and this, too, was let. "Robert Wadelow hath hyred the shoppe at the hygh bridge" and he was charged 6s. 8d. per annum rent.

Certain towns claimed right-of-way over the bridge. In 1582 the toll was let to John Shepperd and Robbe Coward for a period of five years for 10s. per annum. They were to "discharge the toune against the toune of Cambridge or any other privileged toune for any toule taken by them". In 1592 . . . "The toll of the toune bridge is let to Thomas Skotwell and Thomas Shepperd over the water for five years next ensuinge for the clere yearly rent of 10s. 4d. to be paid at Easter alwayes and they to discharge the toune against any privileged toune for taking any other toll than is done". In the latter part of the 16th century the bridge urgently required repairs, an expensive business. Funds were provided in part by loans from principal citizens. Thomas Ladd loaned 20s. and "in lyke manner" William Walsham loaned a similar amount "and more for certyn fyshe on the corte day, 3s. 6d."

Robert Coney and John Mobbe, town surveyors, supervised the repair or rebuilding of the bridge in 1597. More than 50 items were recorded in the parish accounts book concerning the work, the whole amounting to £18 12s. 5d. A few are given here:

Item for 2 days work dragginge the timber from Robert Conyes dore to the bridge, 2s.

Im primis paid to Thomas Suthwold for 6 boat loads of gravell land at Goole Bridge, 2s.

Item pd to the tymber men for 4 boats of tymbre wanting 2 foot, £3 19s. 0d.

Item to the sawyer in all for sawings, 8s.

Item for beere, 3d.

Item for 2 stone of hempe, 3s. 8d.

Item to Nicholas Harte for makyng the same in two ropes, 1s. 4d.

Item to the carpenters in all, £5 17s. 2d.

Item for carryage of woode from Lynwoode and from the pytte, 2s.

Item pd to Tho. Barret for his boat rente, 6d.

Item for fetchynge of a roape from Wimblington and mendynge the same, 1s.

Item for fetchynge of a roape from Wimblington and strewinge the bridge, 4d.

Item to Garner for his pullies, 1s. 4d.

Item for a barrill of beere, 5s. 6d.

Item for sope, butter and tallow, 4d.

Item for 300 of planks lackinge 10 foote, £1 18s. 6d.

Item to Wm. Barryte for carringe the roll from the bridge to the church, 1d.

Item for 17 carte spoakes, 6d.

Item for cartinge of the planks and 4 posts to the bridge, 2s.

At the same time Stutbridge near Town End was repaired, the mender, Mr. Searle receiving 1s. William Suthwold "wrytinge and castinge uppe our book" received 6d. for his pains.

Gravel from Goole Bridge half-way along West End was cast into the river at the existing site and timber was driven upon same. An ancient map named the source of the gravel as "Common called Gold Bridge Pingle" in the centre of which is defined a watercourse from Pease Hill. Lynwood and Coneywood — where lay the remains of a primeval forest — provided the heavy timber for the bridge. These heavy loads had to be conveyed over Stutbridge which had to be strengthened beforehand. This was recognised procedure in the Fens. When the 60 ft long timbers for the construction of Ely cathedral's lantern tower were brought into the district, many wooden bridges had to be reinforced at very considerable cost. Stutbridge formed part of a common near Lynwood and Coneywood at Mill-gate (at present Mill Hill). A yard near Robert Coyne's home, on the site of the present Griffin Hotel, accommodated stocks of timber for use in the construction of the bridge. Some timbers from the old bridge were purchased by March inhabitants, thus defraying expenses. Mr. Petchie living close by paid 1s. 8d. for timber; Edward Amery paid £1 for an item and various other oddments were sold. The new bridge was let to John Shepherd for five years as well as the privilege of washing sheep from another parish and charging 2d. per score of animals. He paid a yearly rent of 13s.

The bridge gave good service for 57 years and in 1654 an order was made for the building of the "great bridge over the River Nean". Total cost of that undertaking was £23 5s. It was let in 1681 for 31s. per annum and in 1723 the yearly rent amounted to £6 15s. The bridge was kept tidy and clean by a paid sweeper, William Neil, who was paid 6d., and who according to the town clerk "never did sweep any more!"

In 1850 a new brick bridge was provided in place of that of timber, then in an advanced state of deterioration. The old bridge was removed together with an unsightly house nearby. The present bridge was erected through the spirited and generous enthusiasm of inhabitants, the trustees of the turnpike and the Middle Level Commissioners. The present bridge cost £600, a third being contributed by the trustees and the remainder defrayed by the Commissioners, one of whom, Charles Culledge, played a notable role. To remove the old bridge and house, inhabitants raised £460, a little short of the amount required. Mr. Culledge headed the subscription list with £50 and eventually the total sum was realised. Mr. Culledge performed the opening ceremony of laying the keystone, and later to celebrate the auspicious occasion a dinner was given at the Griffin Hotel.

An inscription affixed to the bridge reads: "This bridge was rebuilt and the approaches improved by subscriptions from the Middle Level Drainage Commissioners, the Turnpike Trustees, the inhabitants of March and others, through the perseverance and liberalty of Charles Culledge, Esq., 18th September, 1850".

CHAPTER V

Town Guilds

HROUGHOUT the Middle Ages guilds came into being for the benefit of members in times of difficulty. Not all were allied to religious cause but the majority were strongly attached to the Church and were in themselves benefactors to the Church. Guilds were indicative of community opulence and of social standing. Generally speaking, the number of guilds enjoyed by a township said something for the town's wealth. There were seven guilds at March and by that we may deduce that March was a town of some importance. These were dedicated respectively to St. Wendreda, Holy Trinity, St. Anne, St. John the Baptist, St. Christopher, St. Mary, and St. Peter.

The 14th century Guild of St. Wendreda probably had its foundation in the re-establishment of the relic of St. Wendreda among the community and the re-building of St. Wendreda's church to appropriately accommodate the shrine. This gild was unique in that it provided a will:

"Be it remembered that in the town of March within the Isle of Ely, was of old, established a guild in honour of Saint Wyndreda the Virgin, which was removed to the chapel there. And the brothers and sisters of the aforesaid guild have agreed to this rule: that the guild shall provide two wax tapers to burn on festival days before the beir of the aforesaid saint, and one wax taper to burn at the Elevation of Corpus Christi. Moreover, if a brother or sister shall die when at one day's journey from the town aforesaid, the brothers of the guild shall solemnise his or her burial at the charge of the guild — if he or she who died had no means whereby to defray the cost of burial. Also all the brothers and sisters shall meet together at the burial of a brother or sister and shall make an offering for his or her soul; and each of them shall cause one mass to be celebrated, and each of them shall give one farthing to the poor for the soul . . . . of the deceased. Also the brothers shall support the aforesaid guild to their utmost, and, if it shall fall into decay by reason of pestilence or any other source of failure, the goods thereof shall be given towards the fabric of the chapel of March".

Guild certificates refer to this mediaeval institution and clearly state that the relic of St. Wendreda lay enshrined in the chapel. That certain ancient guilds accumulated vast wealth is noticeable in the extravagant treatment of church fabric, as is indicated in the activities of the opulent Guild of Holy Trinity, Wisbech, so imbued with rich possessions that it even maintained flood barriers and was incorporated into the town Corporation.

The March Guild of St. Christopher was one of the more eminent guilds although its officers did not consist of Aldermen, Scabins, Deans, Skyvens and Chamberlains as might be the case at such Hanseatic based towns as King's Lynn and Boston and the inland port of Wisbech. A March man, Mr. Kersey, in his will, bequeathed portions of his wealth to "every gilde within the town of March . . . " An important member of the Guild of St. Christopher, Mr. Kersey's death evoked expressive commemoration in honour of the deceased. All brothers and sisters were summoned to the chapel where each one donated money in memory of Mr. Kersey. The guild altar bore a wax light which was required to burn perpetually. It was a heavy charge on the income of the guild, wax in the 15th and 16th centuries obtainable at 6d. a pound. When a member died, although out of sight he or she was seldom out of mind; it was an important condition that a deceased member's soul be constantly remembered by the guild and dirges, trentals, obits - forms of services - were frequently offered for the repose of the departed. This required the use of the chapel practically every day.

The Guild of St. Christopher of March kept a book in which was written memoranda. Early members were: John Southwold senior, a farmer, and Mary, his wife; John Spencer, shipbuilder and Alice, his wife. Entries were made in contracted Latin in the year 1472. Later entries were recorded in almost unintelligible English, one particular note after modernisation telling us: "Memorandum. The light keeper of St. Christopher, John Walsham, John Neal, Thomas Southwold of Whittlesey End (West End), Thomas Southwold at the Bridge, Richard Coward in the year of our Lord 1495. There remains in John Neal's hands and (in the hands of) Thomas Southold of Whittlesey End for the keeping up of St. Christopher's light 3s. 4d. and 21 lbs. of wax whereof Richard Wright shall pay 1 lb. of wax, John Walsham, John Neal and Thomas Southwold of Whittlesey End the other 1 lb".

Every guild held an annual High Day. Members of St. Christopher's Guild celebrated theirs on the Monday after the Feast of the Epiphany, when funds were entrusted to certain officers. Just before their term of office ended the light keepers had to account for any excess of money or wax. In 1526 the March Guild of St. Christopher comprised of thirty members, not a great number, but of influence and wealth. Each guild had an altar in the chapel of St. Wendreda. The March Guilds apparently had no chapels for individual use as was the case at Wisbech, King's Lynn and Boston where guilds were builders in their own rights. The practice at March was for each guild to erect its respective altar before a pillar in the nave. The altars had colourful drapes and back cloths and candles burned upon them or nearby. The light keepers attended the altars and the candles every day according to requirements, such as honouring obligations to deceased members. These obligations could last from a few weeks to several months, generally depending on financial bequests. The high altar was something apart - the holy of holies - and the shrine of St. Wendreda had special significance, too.

THE RELIC OF ST. WENDREDA

The Guilds of March exercised considerable influence upon the town and in particular the chapel especially benefited by guild contributions in the event of fabric restoration and rebuilding. The church tower was erected in about 1380 and it could well be that the Guild of St. John the Baptist was instrumental in its construction, a boss in the groined passage beneath displaying the saint's emblem, an eagle. In the event of major restoration all guilds were involved, and it is certain that the return of the relic of St. Wendreda to March involved the town guilds who united to put their full measure of resources behind the enlargement and embellishment of the chapel. The little Norman-cum-Early English church was hardly a noble monument to the saint's memory. Indeed there is evidence that the building was in a state of deterioration. A major rebuilding programme was devised and took place prior to 1342. This was principally to make the chapel more worthy of accommodating the relic and to enlarge the building in accordance with the town's growth.

From the inception of the relic being enshrined within the restored chapel and throughout the following two centuries the chapel was constantly being enriched: a tower and south aisle had already been added together with a north porch towards the end of the 14th century; the south porch was added in 1528 this being the final addition. Both aisles were pulled down in the 16th century and rebuilt with the addition of the existing very fine windows. The culmination of all this however was the complete replacement of the clerestorey, a multi-window structure specifically designed to accommodate and shed light on one of the finest timber roofs in the world. This magnificent addition with its one hundred and eighteen angel figures and extras in the form of martyrs and disciples - half life size - was the perfect memorial to the remains of the saint enshrined beneath it. Had the shrine not existed it is doubtful that such a splendid work would have taken place at March. Expert opinion hails the roof as the finest of its kind in Europe.

March stood to gain a great deal from the presence of the saint's relic, which, like others in the land attracted hundreds of pilgrims. The shrine was conveniently positioned between two major reliquaries within the great monasteries at Ely and Peterborough. There were also the monasteries of Thorney, Crowland and Ramsey, much visited places, housing numerous relics. The hand of St. Etheldreda still survives, being displayed in a reliquary kept within Ely's Roman Catholic church. The relic of St. Wendreda had been removed from March to Ely before the Norman Conquest and was well patronised by the faithful. Time passed and the peace of the Isle of Ely was shattered repeatedly by Danish incursions, the raiders favouring religious establishments. Ely, Thorney, Peterborough, Ramsey and Crowland were prime targets and inhabitants put to the sword and buildings raised to the ground. In the 11th century the Saxons organised themselves to contain and resist the Scandinavian invaders.

In 1016 a formidable army of Danes landed on the Essex shore and the Saxon army commanded by Edmund Ironside marched to oppose it. Ironside desperately needed a convincing victory and he attempted to enlist the powers of heaven to that end. The Saxon commander entreated Aelsi, abbot of Ely to allow the relic of St. Wendreda to be brought to him that it might precede the Saxon army to the battlefield. The abbot had nothing to lose for he was anxious as anyone that the heathen Danes suffer defeat. Four monks carried the relic and preparations were made for the battle which took place on St. Luke's Day near the village of Assundon (Ashington) in Essex. It turned out to be a total disaster for the Saxons, the hoped-for miracle failing to transpire - at least not in the way expected. A chronicler wrote: "There was never a more deadly wound given to the English nobility than on that fateful day". Prayerful entreaties were in vain and the bearers of the relic joined the mass of Saxon soldiers grotesquely prostrate on the field. Hundreds died that day before the furious onslaught of the Danes led by their able leader, Canute. The heathen victors seized the coffin encrusted with precious gems and carried it in triumph to their leader.

Canute was not without compassion. Prisoners told him about the life of St. Wendreda and he was moved. That was the miracle. Filled with remorse at his ways Canute became a Christian, an act emulated by his followers. He ordered that the relic be returned to the Saxons and enshrined at Canterbury (Ibid. 196), where for more than three centuries it rested in the cradle of the English faith. It is not known who or what prompted the ecclesiastical authorities to return the remains of the saint to March. It was, however, an appropriate gesture, the saint having been buried there centuries previously. During the 14th century religious processions were commonplace. Many of these were involved in the removal of bits and pieces of human anatomy from one shrine to another. It is possible that large sums of money were involved in the transfer of relics to places better suited to them. The chapel at March had undergone transformation and all was ready for the saint to be enshrined within. The perpendicular structure seen today can be regarded as a shrine in itself, inspired by the saint's return and lavished with mens handiwork to that end '. . . from the peculiar squints beneath the tower to allow passers-by to observe the shrine without entering, to the magnificent angel ceiling which includes the figure of St. Wendreda and that of St. Etheldreda of Ely. When the relic was returned in 1343 - the year of the Indulgence granted by Pope Clement VI at Avignon, it was enclosed within a stone or wood reliquary, and set in a convenient position so as to allow the faithful and visiting pilgrims to pray before it and possibly even to touch the shrine. All this was in accordance with the Indulgence . . . "Being therefore desirous that the Chapel of the Virgin Saint Wendred at March in the Diocese of Ely should be frequented with condign honours and held in continual veneration by Christ's faithful people . . . " The Indulgence applied to all that came to the chapel in devotion, prayer and pilgrimage until it was abruptly ended by the Dissolution.

It is conceivable that March became a one-night stop for weary pilgrims making the slow journey to Walsingham, Norfolk. The physical presence of March's very own saint undoubtedly acted as a fillip upon the parish coffers and this helped to bestow upon the chapel and town those covetted "condign honours". Those two hundred years of saintly influence were unquestionably a memorable period in the town's long history. The end came with a visit in the mid 16th century of the King's Commissioners and with them came desecration and destruction of great works of art to the end of reform. Monasteries were prime targets but no town nor village escaped lightly. Guild brethren were dispossessed and every March guild ceased to function with the national trend. Roman Catholic institutions were plundered and expunged from the life of the parish. Every item silver and gold plate, furniture and other properties fell into the commissioners hands, but happily March guild hall, renamed "toune house" was saved and presented to the parishioners for general use. It was a valuable and useful building as was another edifice, the "treasure house" near St. Wendreda's church.

THE TOUNE HOUSE

The Manor map of 1601 provides a clue as to what the guildhall looked like. It stood near the churchyard and had walls of clay in the best fen tradition. Two stories high, the structure separated by a narrow yard from a smaller building was roofed with timber and layers of fen reed. Someone scratched an entry in the churchwardens book in 1552 that John Thickpenny acted as "farmar to the toune house". He rented the place at an annual payment of 10s. 4d. William Coward later held it for 13s. 4d. The former guildhall was probably built in the 14th century and was crudely constructed, held together by strong framework. It was an important building, second only to the church (manors excepted) and survived in its new role for more than a century.

Influential March families hired the toune house and it was often used for the traditional wedding breakfast, such occasion introducing touches of revelry and colour to otherwise drab surroundings. Couples walked arm in arm down the reed strewn nave of the chapel, smiled upon by Nicholas Stutewile, curate for more than 40 years in which time his hand recorded in the "Regester Booke of Marche" hundreds of baptisms, weddings and funerals. What a marvellous congregation the couples had to bless them on their way to married bliss. Relatives and friends on the one hand and above them seemingly the archway of heaven itself - the glorious assembly of angel figures and musicians and martyrs and disciples which created much prayerful wonder among the beholders and does so to this day. The Church was impartial to all who were wed within its physical confines but once outside the couples fell distinctly into different categories. Daughters and sons of less influential parents, bathed in rapturous joy as was their right contented themselves with a breakfast of sorts in a humble parental abode, surrounded by the genuine kindness of relatives and friends who supplied all the culinary items necessary for the purpose as well as sweetmeats, nosegays and aromatics to fortify the inner man and sweeten prevailing bliss to limit-less horizons. The couples' way was strewn with flowers. Neither did excited helpers neglect to make and hang the bridal garland in the chapel. A wedding of the poor usually exceeded the stereotyped pattern of the wealthy with a community awareness completely unlimited in help and oneness. Somehow musicians were found to jolly things along.

Several alder trees thrived in the yard adjoining the toune house. These were sometimes a nuisance and John Quine felled them in 1569. He used the wood to good effect but had to pay 13s. 4d. for them. The tenant had a problem at that time; the building urgently needed repair and John Taylor, the town's odd-job man was burdened with additional responsibility - he had to "repayre all tymbar". Repair was needed again in 1577 when the toune house was in such a state of deterioration that major restora-tion could no longer be ignored. The call went out to March craftsmen who were allocated tasks to that end. Two childers of lime cost 12s. and Frances Tedmunt received 3s. for bearing it up. The smith received a similar amount for making a clasp.

John Taylor was the senior worker and supervised all work connected with the restoration, being paid 6s. 8d. for five days and "his man fower days' work". Thomas Coward supplied sand and clay (1s. 3d.) and Hugh Coney carried stones to the site for 1s. Henry Tompson, the assistant workman received 1s. 9d. for three days work and 2s. 6d. went into the pocket of Thomas Browne skilled in roof repairs. Three spars cost 1s. 3d., three stude 1s. and "for ij hundreth of bordar 5s. 8d. and for the carryinge of it all from Brandon 1s. 6d.".

After the toune house had been cleared up and a bit of decor added it opened its doors to parishioners and served them for 30 years with the minimum of maintenance. The rent was increased to 14s. in 1579 "reserving allwayes to the toune the use of the house at the brydalls and other meetings . . . " Inflation was a problem and it became necessary to let the building for additional purposes. In 1581 Robert Pette, a weaver, hired the premises on a temporary basis until a new kitchen had been provided, he then moving into the parlor above for a rent of £1 6s. 8d. "provided alwayes that yf the toune do need the kytchen and oven for any other necessytyes, then he do geve place for that tyme". Mr. Pette did not give way too frequently, there being an average of about 10 bridals a year.

It seemed a successful venture and the town fathers considered letting the premises as a school. Thus in 1592 part of the building was converted into a day school ". . . the toune kytchen with the yard thereunto appertayning and the use of the hall to teach in, using it and keeping it clenely". William Southolde Clarke, curate, taught young March children and received a small fee to supplement his meagre stipend. He did not stay long and the tenure was transferred in 1593 to George Brady for £1 11s. per annum.

In 1602 the kitchen and yard was let to Thomas Wheat and William West for 13s. 4d. "so that they shall not hacke nor hew wood nor keep any cattle in the yard from Hallowmas (November 1st) to Easter". A second school was opened in the first decade of the 17th century under Mr. Frears who had the use of the "geale hall . . . and the little chamber next the kytchyn with the upper chamber and the little pingle over against William Hardy, and he is to wryte and find parchment at his own charge and paper for all things needful for the town of March".

More repairs were carried out in 1608, John Hurton of Upwell taking the matter in hand "with 3,000 of reed for the toune house" and laying charge to March the sum of £2 10s. 4d. Later, the building became a shop and part of it accommodated the town's armour. The shop was run by Thomas Bowles on condition that he "skower, dress and make all the toun armour yearlie hereafter for the rent of 13s. 4d." The Constable was actually responsible for the armour but it was not job to maintain it. In addition to the toune house the residents of March enjoyed the benefit of more shops at their disposal, the treasure house in which valuable items were kept, an almshouse and a clock house. The almshouse which was first mentioned in 1622 stood near Bridge Green (Broad Street) and the residents witnessed the drovers taking animals to the watering place.

March Devil r. blk. shy
IN ROOF AT ST. WENDREDA'S

Early Victorian House, West End, March

The White Horse, West End, is partly 17th century

The 17th century Ship Inn, March

Bank House, West End, March, in course of restoration

St. John's Church, March

The River Nene and Park, March

Rivercraft and Reflections, March

Commemorative Fountain, Broad Street, March

Soldier of the First World War, Broad Street, March

Mediaeval Steeple, St. Wendreda's Church, March

The elegant Steeple of Station Road Cemetery, March

St. Peter's Church, March

A busy Saturday scene in High Street, March

March, as seen from the tower of St. Wendreda's church

Knight's End, March

Riverside Gardens, March

For Town and Country

N the previous chapter mention is made of the town armoury. Every town had some means of maintaining its boundaries and for that reason it was necessary that fit and able men attire themselves in armour and familiarise themselves with weapons and be ready to defend their town should the need arise. It was possible too that they would be required to repel an invasion, and if the King or Queen had need of them for defence or for a foreign incursion, they would form a suitable army. There is nothing to suggest that March ever experienced attack by unwelcome visitors, but had an hostile force approached the town it would have discovered that by reason of the town's street plan, intersected by a ribbon work of ditches, the community presented a natural fortress. March was cut in half by the river and high marsh between the bridge and Stone Cross necessitated the use of the dubious Causeway. The outlying fen formed a natural moat, impenetrable in places.

There were few buildings between the bridge and the Stone Cross. Where now we have High Street with its assortment of Georgian and Victorian buildings, formerly this stretch was called Hie Dyke from the existence of The Hythe an ancient waterway now enclosed to the rear of and in certain instances running beneath shops in the High Street. North of the river were lanes parallel to the waterway: Whittle-end (West End) and Outward-end (Nene Parade) also called at one time Well-end. This was the most important area of the town with considerable business off the river. Here near the river was the anciently established secondary community of Mercheford north of which sprawled Norwoodside. Common shared by Mercians and Wisbechians alike. The winding track from the bridge was used mostly by shepherds and drovers. It is known as Robingoodfellow Lane, probably after a national hero. This lane is one of the oldest in March and probably dates to the 13th century. The only other road in the town with a date to it – Burrowmoor Road – was cut out in 1546 to give access to Beremere Fen and fisheries. To make this road cost the churchwardens just eleven shillings. Elwyn Road is a flowery version of the former ancient Elin district of March. Deerfield, Dartford and Badgeney, Peas Hill and Estover all derive from ancient areas.

March was not always on good terms with neighbouring towns – Wisbech in particular. Inevitably Wisbech and March men came together on Norwoodside where herds and flocks grazed. It seems that the two communities were at loggerheads on more than one occasion and that the disputes came to a head over sheep and temporarily ended after the Bishop of Ely had intervened. In 1591 bondsmen and tenants of Wisbech went to Norwoodside as usual to tend their animals and discovered a number of sheep maimed and mutilated. Accusing fingers indicated March men as the culprits but they denied having anything to do with it. A man of March, oddly enough a butcher, declared: "We did not do this thing. The Wisbech men had got themselves too merry and killed and maimed their own sheep to the end and purpose of slandering the town of March".

In his role the Bishop presided over a great many things concerning his diocese and was often besought to settle disputes. March and Wisbech apparently vied with each other at the top of the list! It all proved too much for the eminent gentleman who declared his intentions against March in no uncertain manner. Can we not hear his stentorian voice echoing along the corridors of time, dictating to his scribe who duly forwarded the missive to the churchwardens: "I am sorrye to heare that ye are so stoute, so disordered and so lawlesse people, that neyther the order of me and my counsell can stay you. I understand ye fall to yor old practyse, please yorselves in yor own devises, go contraye to yor oune agremente, and pynne yor neighbours cattell. Sithe ye be at that poynte I ensure you what the law will gyve me that I intende to use roundelye agaynste you. Say not that you have not had warnyng. So fare ye well. From Downham ye viijth of April. Yors, R. Ely".

March boundaries were extensive. To the west they extended almost to Coates and a man from that village who accidently trespassed beyond the boundary to fish, was seen, warned and fined by March churchwardens. Several years previously in 1542 March fenreves (commoners with rights) impounded Elm cattle which had strayed over the boundary near Elm dyke. They were set free on imposition of a heavy fine and the matter duly recorded in the churchwardens' book. Parochial boundaries were very uncertain and it was common for two or more townships to claim the free use of outlying marsh and common grounds and many were the occasions when Wisbech, Elm and March became embroiled in these matters. How could a marsh be marked for boundaries, especially when they were subject to geological changes? Tempers flared and threats were made. It was probably as well that March kept its armoury in readiness!

Able-bodied men living at March were obliged to train frequently in military skills. They were perfectly familiar with that most feared of weapons - the English long bow, and handled powder and ball with cautionable knowledge. Swords and daggers were not mere ornaments but were kept scrupulously clean and razor sharp as befits their purpose. It was essential as well as traditional that every town and village in the realm provide arms for certain of its people, principally for use in defence. To this end nothing surpassed the resolute spirit of the English who, rightly or wrongly, with the aid of sharpened shafts and sword and axe had commanded a great deal of respect throughout Europe. By ancient law re-enacted in 1571, "every man under 60 years of age, shall have a long bow of yew, and every man having a man child or men children in his house shall provide for all such being at the age of

seven years and above and till they shall come to the age of 17 years
a bow and two shafts to learn them and bring them up in shooting. And
after such men shall come to the age of 17 years, every one of them
shall provide and have a bow and four arrows continually for himself,
at his proper costs and charges, or else of the gift and provision of
friends, and shall use the same as afore is rehearsed".

By 1550 gunpowder was already well established but the English bow
continued to be a much feared and trustworthy weapon. In accordance
with the Act, bowstaves "shall be three fingers thick and squared, and
seven feet long, and to be got up well polished and without knots".
An Act passed in 1542 decreed that every village and town maintain a
pair of butts, and "no person above the age of 24 shall shoot with the
light arrow at a distance under 200 yards". March had a field in which
was placed butts for men to practice at the town's expense.

1552 - Payd for ye butts 1s. 8d.
1568 - Payd for a case for a sheaf of arrows, etc. 5s. 6d.

March archery ground of about one rood was let to Laurence Wenden
and Jeremy Chandler for nine years at a yearly rent of 4s. Eventually
the bowstave was superseded by musket and ball, devices sometimes as
deadly to the handler as the target. Ancient guns were lar less re-
liable, and much slower to reload, than the silent steel-tipped shaft
the heavier kind of which were capable, in the hands of an expert
archer, of penetrating armour plate and transfixing a man's leg to his
horse at a distance of 200 yards.

The following accounts relate to the armoury of March:

1557 - Paid to John Sheppherd when he bought the gunne, 7s. 6d.
1580 - Paid to Wm. Twaytly for a sword and dagger, 6s. 8d.
1622 - Payd to John Coward for a dish of fish bestowed upon Sir
       Richard Coxe when the town was charged with new muskets,
       13s. 6d.

The following accounts were entered about 1600:

Item - One corslet belongyng to certain of the subsidy men.
Item - One colliner with the flaskyt and a tutch box.
Item - One corslet belongyng to the toune.
Item and one cote of plate remayning in the hands of Wm. Coward
       de Bageney.
Item - belongyng to the toune one almayne reyneit (this is a puzzle)
Item - A bow and a sheaf of arrows and a sword.
Item - One other almayne reyneit (?) and a seutt and a colliner with
       the flaskyt and touch boxe and a sword.

The colliner was a heavy musket supported by a tripod, and the
corslet a breastplate usually strapped to a backplate.

BATTERY HILLS

Cavalry Barn, Battery Hills and Hill Fields are time honoured March names possessing strong military implications. Not a thing remains above the surface - except a few irregular earthworks - to substantiate a former military post or fortress at March. Yet evidence has been found of a military camp at March before 1650. The area in which the fortress is said to have been sited lies slightly to the east of Neale-Wade school and events leading to its possible establishment is worth commenting upon. The Parliamentary cause drew its initial strength from the Eastern Counties. This was due to the formation of the Eastern Counties Association with the great Fenman, Oliver Cromwell, soon to be at its head. In the Isle of Ely loyalty for the opposing sides was fairly evenly divided.

The Isle of Ely presented a natural buffer protecting the Association's north flank. The King, too, realised its importance and at the outset of hostilities attempted to wrest it from Parliament and give the Royal army access into Norfolk and Suffolk. The Fen soldiers, rough-clad initiators of what was later to be known as the Model Army, a most efficient, disciplined force, defended the Isle not only against the King but from the enemy within. Anxious moments did arise, Royalist sympathisers creating disturbances at Ely which resulted in the cathedral being closed for 17 years. The sizeable Royalist faction at Wisbech could not be disregarded either. When the King's army gained early victories the Isle garrison was placed on alert and constant patrols made.

The Marquis of Newcastle, for the King, drew near the Isle with a large regular army and Captain Dobson of the Isle's Parliamentary force, a highly capable officer of some severity, rounded up Wisbech Royalists and locked them in the large parish church until the crisis had passed. Where did March come in this? The slight protrusion on which the town is strategically placed offered an ideal position from which to direct security operations. It allowed good access to other towns as well as Ireton's Way, then a new military road built for the use of Parliament troops (this is the Mepal Straight) which rose at its east end to the prominence on which Ely stands. It was recognised practice during the Civil War for both sides to requisition suitable buildings. It is not improbable that a large building at March was acquired for the Parliamentarian presence. Cavalry Barn and Battery Hills indicate a connection. Just off Barker's Lane there were at one time ground irregularities and stone blocks buried in the soil were found. Older residents recalled earth embankments and ditches in a grassed area known as Hills Field.

In the summer of 1849 a March man, Captain Hamilton, made extensive excavations on the site, this revealing evidence of a fortress of some kind. The hills were in fact circular mounds, one at the time of excavation, presenting itself in a fair state of repair. Remains of a, timber stockade were also exposed. This evidence defined what appeared to be the outline of a fortress having its main front facing north with at least three circular mounds suitable for setting up cannon. One of the mounds was 20 feet wide. The interior of the site apparently contained the foundations of a large building. The west and north walls were of large stone and the south and east walls of brick. To the north the main entrance was approached by way of a drawbridge over the fosse, and the remains of a road led directly to St. Wendreda's church. The discovery in the ruin of pottery and tobacco pipes of the 17th century strengthen the supposition that a building here had been converted into a bastion for defensive or alternative purposes.

It has been suggested on more recent excavation that the "hills" were no more than "practice fortifications" as the surviving earthworks seemed irregular. When the site was inspected by Captain Hamilton more than 150 years ago, much more presented itself to the eye and according to him the site was utilised by some military group. Around the area certain objects relevant to a troop of cavalry having lodged in the vicinity have occasionally been found. The Reverend C. E. Walker, M.A., author of "Records of a Fen Parish" suggests that the earthworks were manned for the King. This, in the writer's opinion, was unlikely. While March had its Royalist sympathisers they were in no position to display active interest as the Isle of Ely was well patrolled by Parliamentary soldiers who in no way would have tolerated a Royalist outpost in their circuit. It could well be that the fortress was commanded by Captain Dobson for Parliament. This man who lived at Outwell was in command of 70 cavalrymen the troop being financed by the inhabitants of the Isle. March was heavily taxed during the war, the sum of £3 extracted from the town in 1648. The following entry is of note:

> Received by William Neale of Mr. Girlinge the sum of £10 which is part of the £14 3s. 4d. allowed to the town by the Committee for monies spent by the town in times of alarm.

This may be a reference to some military adventure affecting the town. Colonel Fairfax of Colchester Garrison had expressed doubts as to the preparedness of the Isle of Ely in the early stages of the Civil War. It was for that reason that a force of cavalrymen under Captain Dobson was billeted in the Isle of Ely (as I think at March) the town, very central and convenient was ideally strategically situated. The object of the garrison – to show the Parliament flag – included regular patrols to Ely, Whittlesey and Wisbech and disenchant any ideas from the Isle's Royalist sympathisers. There was probably a great deal of activity at March during the siege of King's Lynn held for a time by the Royalists. Oliver Cromwell stayed a little while at Needinghall, Emneth, and must have passed through March on more than one occasion, being particularly interested in Wisbech, a small Parliamentary troop camping at Three Horseshoes, near the town. Captain Hamilton suggested that the fortress at March was a crenellated building. It had a moat and a drawbridge – in fact a typical defensive layout of the Middle Ages. Could it have been the original Eastwood Manor?

When Charles II assessed the country from the Throne he may have
thought that the rigours and discipline of the Puritans had been more
than enough and he decided upon a "merry" attitude and merry living.
Even so, the Republic under Cromwell had raised the country from a
soft position to one well respected by foreign powers. The Restoration
did not soften financial burdens which the Commonwealth had imposed
upon communities. March, in line with other towns in the Isle, had to
pay special rates, it seems because the Isle had supported the Parliamentary cause! To rub it in, much of the extra money went to the relief
of indigent cavaliers who had faithfully served the monarch's unfortunate
father. A destitute widow of Doddington, whose wounded husband had died
after coming out of the army, having been a prisoner of war in a
Parliamentarian camp, received some compensation to help her and her
four children to cope with difficult times. Other cavaliers from our
historic little Fen island who died in service for the King were Martin
Bingham, March; Thomas Bavin, Doddington; William Burkett, Doddington;
and William Thomason, Wimblington. The widows of these men each
received a pension of £5 per annum.

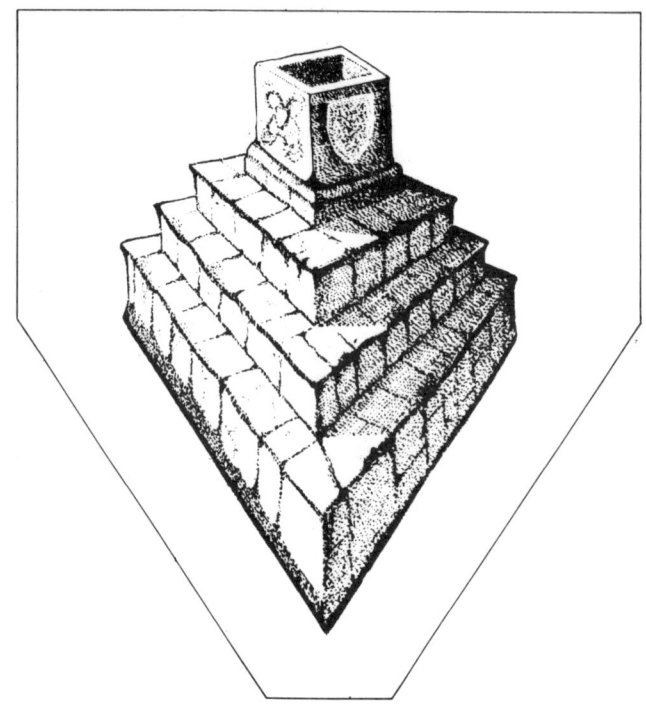

CHAPTER VII

The Stone Cross

HE controversial base which supported a shaft bearing a cross, calvary or some religious emblem has stood for several centuries in The Avenue, approximately half way between St. Wendreda's church and the present Market Place. The stepped base dates from between 1450 and 1520. There are indications that it was a preaching cross erected by an order of preaching friars, several such orders then existing at Cambridge. The friars generally attired in coarse black, brown or white apparel, according to their order, were beheld in a vindictive light by parochial clergy who would not tolerate them in churches or even churchyards. The friars were regarded by Sir Priest as a confounded nuisance who seemed determined to undermine the authority of local priests. Undeterred, the great friary Orders sent out their members to preach the Gospel in a more direct fashion and held services in towns and villages, erecting stone pulpits in the form of crosses in the most convenient places. The friars provided counter attractions at country fairs and were popular for their jolly attitudes and equally adept when in came to verbal fireworks and forthright address. What tales these ancient wayside crosses could tell!

Friary Orders were careful to erect the crosses as near as possible to the place where markets were held. At the beginning of the 15th century March extended a limb towards Mercheford where a great deal of commerce would be found along the riverside. This expansion followed the ridge along the present Avenue. It is the writer's opinion that the Stone Cross may well mark the site of the town's mediaeval market, halfway between Merche and Mercheford. Certainly the vanished stone shaft supported a carving which was considered to be idolatrous and for that reason removed. It was almost certainly a wayside pulpit for preaching friars. This is substantiated in that the shaft had religious significance and suffered in the same way as hundreds of similar stepped pulpits, at the time of the Dissolution and during the Reformation. Perhaps the same hands that pulled down the rood loft in the church deprived stone base in The Avenue of its shaft with cross or calvary? If the structure had been purely a market cross as at Lavenham, in Suffolk, which is almost identical to the base at March, with no so-called "offending" figure, then the Fen town's example would probably have escaped mutilation.

One feels justified in accepting that the Stone Cross was the focal point of a meeting place, Merche and Mercheford inhabitants meeting halfway to purchase market ware, sometimes sermonised by a friar making use of the stepped base with the stone figure on the shaft reminding everyone what it was all about. Market crosses were little different to preaching crosses. At the end of the 15th century at least 5,000 preaching and market crosses existed in the country. The cross at March was one of the last to be erected, few being built after 1510. They were eventually replaced by crosses of a more practical and worldly nature, usually named after necessary commodities such as butter and wool; roofs were erected above them supported by pillars. Thus came into being the familiar type of open market seen nowadays. A notable example of a 17th butter cross is that at Whittlesey. The river at March then being an important commercial waterway influenced the town fathers and the lord of the manor at Doddington provided the present market site in 1670.

The ancient Stone Cross had played its part in the life of the town and with the making of a better road over the high marsh between the Stone Cross and the river it lost its identity and became an object of curiosity, cloaking itself with mystery to succeeding generations, the youthful element claiming that the devil could be heard rattling his knife and fork in the shaft recess! A March man, Mr. Crowson, once informed the writer that he deciphered a date on the stone base. Alas, the stonework is too worn to recognise much detail. It is a common style conforming from the mid 14th century to the opening years of the 16th century. The worn shields and geometrical designs are reminiscent of around 1500. Weary with age, but well restored, March Stone Cross is a rare thing indicative of those distant times when priest and friar vied for people's souls while the bemused inhabitants searched for bargains. The obelisk below was called the market Butter Cross.

March Market Place, c 1750. Market Established 1670.

CHAPTER VIII

Merrymaking and the Reformation

ERRY-MAKING was a means of temporarily forgetting stress and strain of everyday living. Church festivals were something to look forward to but these occasionally had a morbid aspect. The Churchwardens' book of 1553 tells of a visit to March by very important people. The town, a little apprehensive as to what it would gain - or lose - by the visit deemed it a good thing to treat the visitors with the utmost courtesy. The individuals acting for the King's Commissioners repaid the town's kindness by seizing valuable church plate and anything else of value. They made an inventory of other things. It was an infamous occasion in this sense at least. Precious silver and other goods accumulated over the centuries were removed from the church and treasure house, but a few items were not disclosed and remained in the town. Even so, the town fathers put on a little merry-making in the hope of getting the inquisitive visitors into a good mood.

It appears that in 1553 March had a first class cateress. We do not know her name, except that her husband was "Sam". The scribe entered in his book that the good lady was commissioned to sweeten the very important people with her excellent gastronomical preparations.

    1553 - Item to Sam's wife for two feasts makynge the first day
           and the last xxxiijs.

What was this late mediaeval menu? All was entered by the scribe including the cost: "Beif 6d., mutton and lam 4s. 8d., a capon and chykens 2s., and warpe of salt fishe 3s., and fresh fyshe 8s" Robert Fysher was given 5s. for providing mutton and veal and a Mr. Barret 2s. 6d. for a barrel of beer. Umfre Brown's wife received 1s.4d. for the chickens and bread accounted for 1½d. The feast was held in the recently acquired Guildhall of St. Christopher and our very helpful friend John Taylor who served in the kitchen went home 1s. 6d. richer. It was probably the first event in the guildhall under the new arrangements. Other guildhalls in the town, including that of St. John the Baptist were later privately sold.

March often received visits from important people and it was the custom to present them with gifts. Sometimes these took the form of bribes but one supposes that the beneficiaries, the Lord Bishop, for instance, felt quite happy over these matters.

    1553 - Item for carrying a present to my lord, 2s. 3d.
    1567 - Paid to Robte Coward when he went to my lord with fysh,
           15d.
    1567 - Paid to John Harker for carrying a present to my lord, 2d.

Wildfowl and fish were an inescapable part of a Fen person's diet. These were plentiful and cheap. Lamb and mutton made a nice change, but venison was a rarity and expensive, frequently imported from Huntingdonshire and Northants. Godwits were very popular, these resembling snipe. They, too, found a place in the Churchwardens' book.

1554 - Item paid for half-dozen godwits, 6s.
1558 - Item paid for 15 godwits, 8s.
1558 - Item paid for the carriage of the said godwits, 1s. 3d.

A "styck" of fish cost 8d. in 1568. In 1578 William Bunking was paid 5s. for obtaining a load of fish and delivering it to Sir Francis Hynd and Master Sergeant Shoot (an appropriate name!). Sir Francis lived at Eastwood Hall and was an eminent local person holding the office of magistrate. March seems to have been very merry when it came to King-making. The accession of James I was a right royal occasion, gallons of local brewed ale flowing into the bellies of the March men.

1603 - Paid for ij barrels of beere for joy of the Kinge, 8s.

The Prince's coming to England was another joyous event. This marked the return of the Prince of Wales, later ill-fated Charles I, from Spain. This cultured prince started well but the taxes he imposed did not endear himself to his subjects. Oliver Cromwell eventually had him beheaded. When Oliver too deceased March did not celebrate his successor and son, Richard, a shy weak young man who was far more at home with his farm at Wicken. It was generally recognised that the Monarchy under some sort of control was best for England. And so when on the accession of Charles II March young people skipped and tripped merrily, the bells rang and the river men sang:

1661 - Pd to Thomas Shepheard for colour for the maypole, 10s.
      - Pd to William Nelson for painting of it, 5s.
      - Spent upon the Coronation day, £2 3s. 2d.

Church bells truly came into their own on royal occasions. The poetry of English steeples are embodied in the tradition of bellringing and bells have been heard at March for at least seven centuries. After the accession of Elizabeth I the smallest bells of St. Wendreda's church were sold. Those that remained rang out on St. Hugh's Day, November 17th, 1558 to commemorate the enthronement of the great Queen and they echoed over the rooftops of March all day and throughout the night. The ringers rang the bells on any excuse and their devotion and loyalty was nearly always recognised. In 1566 they rang the bells when the Bishop - "mi lord" - passed through March to preach at Elm. They were given 8d. to purchase beer, but when he came to March, the ringers received only 2d! The Bishop visited the town again in 1571 and a solitary ringer was given 6d. for his efforts. In 1577 the bell boys did well to receive 3s. for "Quenes Day", the bells being rung all through the night. In 1593 the ringers received 3d. for ringing on St. Hugh's Day and 1s. 8d. for the ringers' bread and beer.

Other relevant items are:

1593 – Pd to Climent Rogers and Sandon Yedon for 5 days work and
for taking down of the bell and hanging it up again, 5s.
(Alexander was the town's carpenter, living in Whittle-end.)

– Item to Thomas Mayhew for a gallon of beare and pennyworth
of butter, 5d. (Butter was for greasing the bell gudgeons).

– Item pd to Thomas Sheppard for carrying of the bell to
Cambridge and bringing it home again, 2s. 6d.
(The bell had been recast).

It was left to the bellringers to keep the bells in ringable condition, but every precaution was taken that the bells were up to the mark
for special events. Just before the Coronation of James I the ringers
received 5d. for "grese and candell" (lubricating agents). Four hundred
years ago bells were hung on plain bearings and they were hard to swing.
A lot of lard and butter was used to keep them running smoothly. In
1613 the great bell of March was cast, this being the first of several
similar operations at March. The so-called great bell weighed about
12 cwts. It was cast by John Draper of Thetford, who did not have a
particularly good name for his instruments.

1613 – Item spent in charges in going to Thetford and John Neale
wages, 14s.

– Item spent at Thetford in drink after the bell was shott,
2s. 3d. (Shott was to pour the metal in the moulds which
called for celebration, more like the announcement of a
birth. Before the bell was hung in the tower it was draped
in lace and christened).

– Item spent at Pearches(?) at weighing the bell, for straw
and rudder-hilt. (The latter was a device for shaping the
moulds). 1s. 2d.

– Item spent in hanging the bell up – and in bread and beere,
2s. 2d.

The actual cost of casting this bell was 2s. More than 30 years'
later a similar operation set the church back by £5 2s. 6d. and the
traditional drink 5s. 6d. A further 9s. 6d. was incurred on the parish
when the transport broke down. Inflation was then very high due to the
Civil War. The present ring of six bells cast at Osborn's foundry at
Downham Market, Norfolk, was installed for about £450. A similar job
at the present time would involve an expenditure of about £20,000.

Merry-making was one thing and introduced a good sense of community spirit in the little Fen town. Few inhabitants went further
than Wisbech, Wimblington and Doddington. The Church, too, engendered
a togetherness and supported various feasts. Prior to the Dissolution
the Church was in fact the focus point of community exercise, a

prerogative upon the inhabitants which was not always welcome. In the 1540's the majority of March citizens were contented to let things stay as they were, but there were others who knew that changes were coming and were willing to support such changes. The friars were having hostile questions thrown at them and Sir Priest knew of certain unquiet in the town. The Dissolution of the monasteries was the signal to usher in the new era which was to affect March and the rest of the country for at least two centuries.

ALL CHANGE

What could we expect to find if we had entered the ancient chapel of St. Wendreda in its unreformed state? Incense invaded the nostrils and iron frames stood at convenient places for the faithful to affix candles. "God's lyght" burns night and day, illuminating the several images. The priest attired himself with a rochet, alb and sleeved surplice. He was a resplendent figure when he finally donned a colourful cape of brown, green, blue and gold. He had to be knowledgeable as he had to cope with the Breviary and Grayill, service books, and the Missal permenantly rested upon the altar. Should the Bishop attend, then the Pontifical was brought out and another book probably used more than the rest was called the Pie, a reference to all the other works. The congregation could not read holy writ. Indeed they were not allowed to.

Although the storm clouds of the Dissolution were gathering, March did not seem to be greatly affected as late entries to the churchwardens books testify:

1542 - Payd to the goldsmith for a pyx and crismatory of silver, iiij li. (The latter was used at baptisms).
- Payd for makyn lxi of waxx at Candlemas, vijd.
- Payd for a case to carry the pyxxes, ijd.
1543 - Payd for xvi ellns of cloth for rochytts, xs. vjd.
- Payd for waxx at Sturbridge fayer, xxijs.
(Sturbridge Fair was held at Cambridge).
1544 - Payd in advance for a sanctus bell, js. viiijd.
1547 - Payd for mendynge the bannver (banner) on Ascension Day, ijd.

Change came to March quite simply. It was in the form of a Bible.

Item. for ye bybyll, xs. viijd.

The Great Bible or Bishops' Bible was decreed by Henry VIII to be set up in every parish church and chapel. It was printed in English and anyone with education was free to read it. But the old ways lingered on. Latin was still used in the church and unintelligible prayer heard by the illiterate. The Easter Sepulchre is erected and a roster of parishioners "watched" the emblem of the Resurrection, being paid 9d. for that privilege. Henry VIII died and his son, Edward, ascended the Throne. This gave greater momentum to the Reformation and huge monastic buildings were being taken down in order to use materials for other purposes. The images within the chapel were taken down and destroyed. Those people engaged in this task received 3d. but to the credit of all concerned not a single figure in the angel roof was touched. The successful conclusion of the changes signalled some sort of celebration, and the town's able cateress was again called upon to provide victuals:

Item to Sam's wyfe for drynkynge the first time the emags war plucked downe, js. Od.
Item to Thomas Payne and John Andrew for berying gers (images) furch of church, xd.

How colourless and drab the chapel of St. Wendreda must have looked after the Dissolutionists had had their way. Nothing is mentioned as to what happened to the shrine containing St. Wendreda's relic. The rood loft with its religious figures still remained, but it was soon to go as was the screen beneath. How was it then that the fine angel roof escaped harm while elsewhere in the country scores of beautiful roofs such as that at Willingham were mutilated? Wherever double hammerbeam roofs survived it was attributable to the high pitch of the structure.

The angel roof at March in itself a remarkable feat of men's skill, adheres to the principles of thrust and counter-thrust. The clerestorey which supports it is pierced by several windows, and thereby weakened. A roof as high pitched as this one would weaken the clerestorey still further, but the jacklegs (between the windows) add more weight and the hammerbeams projecting into the nave, each weighted with a heavy oak figure transfer the lateral thrust into the centre. If the roof had been one of lower pitch, as at Willingham, with a single tier of angels then it would have given itself to the Reformists intentions. To have removed a single figure from the March roof could have caused problems. The people of March were cautious and even the Commissioners recognised the need to preserve the church for worship. Over zealousness was not allowed to cloud logic. Besides, the roof which is regarded as the finest of its kind in Europe, after removal of other adornments in the chapel, forms the crowning glory of an otherwise symmetrical but plain building.

When all things "objectionable" had been removed the chapel interior was whitewashed. One wonders whether successive whitewashings of the walls concealed mediaeval paintings. It was common to paint walls with illustrative pictures which helped the illiterate to understand, and to preserve the paint with applications of white of egg. The Reformation gathered pace:

1550 - Item payd for breakyng down the altar and carrying forth ye stonns, js. Od.

A new wooden communion table replaced the high altar. The parish clerk went to Ely in 1553 to write the inventory and received a shilling. Later the church plate was removed to Ely. A new communion book was obtained from Wisbech for 5s. and a table cloth for the communion table cost 1s. 10d.

Then came an unexpected turn of events. King Edward VI who never had a strong constitution, died and his half sister, Mary, a true adherant to the Papacy, ascended the Throne. The Queen ordered that the newly sown seeds of Protestantism be uprooted and church services revert to the practice of 10 years before. People that stoutly resisted were tortured and many burned at the stake. When the opportunity came the Church of England took vengeance on the Roman Catholics and they too, were introduced to a slow death by fire. Such was the meaning of religion in a land ruled by rack and block. At March as in other places the process of reforming the Church was suspended, and new items purchased in line with Roman ritual. These included a crismatory (3s.), a pyx (2s.) and a "halliwat stooke" (holy water stoup), possibly that set into the south porch; a grayil, high altar and altar cloth were also purchased. The sanctus bell was restored to its cote and a new frame obtained for candles and a chair for the censer. Iron frames were obtained for processional banners and at the same time (1557-8) the organ bellows was repaired. March people must have wondered what was happening. The ecclesiastical turnabout, although sadly steeped in blood, was however shortlived and with the demise of the Queen the Reformation took up the loose ends and continued as strong as ever on course towards the re-establishment of the new look Church.

When the great change first occurred, new churchwardens John Fage and Robert Anderson who had leanings towards new attitudes seem to have carried out their tasks gradually introducing change, including the introduction of the English Prayerbook. On the accession of Mary these two men handed over the offices to Edmund Coney and Roberd Coward who were more familiar (and acceptable) to the old faith and to them fell the duties of restoring full Roman doctrine to St. Wendreda's. Final entries under the Roman Catholic Order at March were thus written:

Item paid for 3 pounds and a quarter of wax, ijs. viijd.
Item paid for the makyng of it, iijd.

On November 7th, 1558, Elizabeth I commenced her reign and with her blossomed the full surge of Protestantism, something not entirely expected and which would have astounded her father who merely wanted to reform the existing Church and putting it to rights. During the early years of the Queen's reign Homilies were purchased for St. Wendreda's and for the final time the high altar was taken away. A temporary communion table was installed and part of the paraphrase - simple explanation of Holy Scripture - was purchased in 1560. Then arose the destroyers of beautiful things, men who let their enthusiasm better their logic, entered the old church and removed the rood loft and its figures fixed onto the chancel arch. The doorway is still there.

1561 - Item to John Taylor for pulling down the rood loft, js.

Nothing was really gained in removing this object. It served to remind the beholder of the very foundation of his faith. Anyway Mr. Taylor made short work of it, removing the figures of Christ crucified, St. Mary and St. John, then he turned his attention to the beam from which on past occasions choristers had sung. From the timber the odd-job man made a footstool for the priest. Stands were supplied by this man for the table end and finally the organ was taken down. With that the new Order had established itself at March.

Many March people looked back with nostalgia to the old days. Living in town were credible families who, while not exactly enthusiastic about the change, did not enjoy seeing the fabric of the chapel pilfered with. In 1528 the nave had been refashioned at considerable expense and the south porch added. People like the Walshams, Southe-wells, Dredemans, Kerseys, Hansarts, Shepherds, Cowards and Coneys did not stand idly by and watch the results of their own and their parents and grandparents benevolence threatened with destruction. All else had to go, but the angel roof - the pride and joy of March - had to be spared if only for practical reasons. Their approach to the Commissioners, with the help of Sam's wife (!) saved the day and to this day the roof remains, a testimony to the former shrine which it protected and the faith of our forefathers. It is interdenominational and nobly portrays the skill, care and eye for detail possessed by the craftsmen of nearly five centuries ago. The Hansart brass with its rare illustration of the Annunciation, too, happily escaped total destruction.

Numerous items were recorded in the churchwardens' book between 1560 - 1588, a few given here:

1560 - Pd to the belman for strewyn ye church, vijd.
      (Strewing the floor with reed and straw)
     - Item pd to James Neill for whitelether for the bells, iis.
     - Payd to Ambrose Seix (Sexton) for mendyng ye church wall
      next Marshalls, vijd.
1565 - Item payd to John Tayler for mendyng of ye beir, xiid.
     - Item pd to widow Harker for lendyng her ladder to the
      church, iiijd.
     - Item pd to John Tayler for mendyng ye bell when John
      Coward was buried, vid.
1568 - Item pd for bred and drincke when we took down ye bells,
     iis.
1569 - Item pd to West (Sexton) for paynting ye cloth in ye
     chancell, xviiid.
1571 - Item for expences when I went to Ely to buy ye communion
     cuppe, ijs. iiijd.
     - Charges layd forth by ye hands of goodman Brode.

"Goodman" was the equivalent of "Master". Master Brode made out accounts concerning cloth or tapestry which from the chancel screen. The object of this was to divide the chancel from the nave and add warmth to the congregation.

1571 - Item to all Masters for xiiij skins thrid bradyngs, xiiijd.
- Item to Hew Byrd for striping ye cloth, xijd.
- Item to John Tayler and Edward Stransome for hangynge up ye nobbs and ye cloth, ijs. iiijd.
1575 - Inprimis to Harry Thompson for makynge ye hedge in ye churchyard, ijs.
1578 - Payd to Lorance Horne and John Hopwood for fetchyng ye stones at Thorney, iijs.
Pd for the stones and a boy to help to lode up.withall, viijd.

Stones from Thorney were undoubtedly obtained from the fabric of the disused abbey there. It was still in the process of being demolished, some of the larger stones taken to Cambridge and incorporated into the colleges being enlarged at the time. The east end of the south aisle of St. Wendreda's church displays signs of repair the use of different stone visible including the upper part of an ogee arch - foreign to March but not to Thorney.

A few more items from that fascinating 16th century March book:

1578 - Pd to Nicholas Huckwell for poynting of the steple, xxxiijs. iiijd.
1579 - Pd to plummynge upon the porch, xviiid.
1580 - Item for paper for to wrightin sertin names, ijd.
- Item for John Joyner for xi days worke about the seats at ix the daye.
- Item more allowed him towards his bed, iiid.
- Item spent at John Neals upon him and them that helped to carry the cloke (clock) to the boette, xiiijd.
1584 - Item for beare which was dronke in the quere (choir), iiid.
1586 - For making of a keye for the chests in the treasurehouse, 8d. (This is believed to be an example of the earliest use of Arabic numerals, not generally in use until 1637).
1588 - Covenanted with the glazier for glassing the Church tyll Lamas next xxs., whereof he hath received xiijs. iiijd.

THE AFTERMATH

"The poor are always with us". Four hundred years ago this was painfully obvious. If we were living then by law of averages we would be numbered with them. Ill-clad, consumptive, undernourished and often seen to be emaciated and devoured by ulcers, these unfortunate people - many thousands thrown to one side by the Dissolution and on-going reformative ideals were alienated by a bewildered society struggling to preserve its existence with dignity. From hovels and hedgerows the poor trekked to villages and towns with their begging bowls. A masterless man was constantly at risk. Having no job identified one as a vagabond. A masterless man was an embarrassment in his native place and he could expect no help from other places. He would be turned away with a penny in his purse rather than put under lock and key and incur greater expense on the parish.

"The Reformation a necessity! What's that to me?" justifiably cried the poor man. "The monasteries fed me, washed me, soothed my sores, gave me a bed. I lay and listened to the Angelus bell and the chanting of the monks. They gave me work in the morning and set me on the road with my stomach full. These places are being pulled down. It is religion to cast me away for ever?" Before the Dissolution of the monasteries the poor had one great hope. Those religious houses welcomed the destitute and sustained and cared for them in return for menial tasks. When they left, the poor had food in their bellies to fortify them on the road to distant monasteries. In the Fens were many such establishments with huge estates where the underprivileged could work for the basic necessities in life. Some towns such as March for instance were enriched by the presence of charitable nuns, tending distressed and poor parishioners. The monasteries ran schools with certain success. The Dissolution and its aftermath wrote finis to all that and the results were catastrophic, sending tremors through the length and breadth of the country for more than two centuries.

Discarded upon the roadsides the poor in their hundreds who had relied for their relief at Ely, Peterborough, Thorney, Crowland, Sawtry and Ramsey, sought fresh fields to replenish their bowls. Along with them went the masterless men, leaning heavily for survival upon villages and towns. There was an economic crisis upon the nation and inhabitants seeing the dead by the roadsides and in church porches, beat their breasts and declared that the Church was finished.

The newly established Church struggled to justify its emergence but for many souls it was too late. It was left to individuals of means to bridge the gap and provide some measure of relief to the poor. Bequeathment of land by wealthy land owners was a helpful means of relief. It was the beginning of the age of the middle classes exemplified by the sturdy yeoman, and was almost as if Divine intervention had localised the miserable poor and that men recognised the need for parochial action. Something had to be done to replace the charitable acts of monastic institutions and the problem was partly alleviated in that every parish learned to recognise and assist its own distressed people. Certain noblemen opened their kitchens to provide soup for those that sat upon their doorsteps. Others gave land. Recorded in the church-wardens book at March:

John Fringe was burd the 21 day of July.

A man of substance, Mr. Fringe was married to Margaret Reynold but had no issue. He was troubled at the plight of March young people and it was his wish to leave his estate at Leverington to the churchwardens of

March, to enable March children to be put out as apprentices:

- 1607 - Paid for our dinners when we went to Wisbech to take
  possession, 7s. 4d.
  - Paid for a fine of recovery of John Fringe's land, £3 4s. 0d.
  - Spent when we did tale the estate of John Fringe's land,
    1s. 0d.
  - For beer and wax at the same time 5d. (wax for sealing the
    agreement).

The land was let to James Laurence for a term of six years from
1647 at an annual sum of £9. The occupier "is not to plow but if he
plows he is to pay 20s. extra every year he plows". This and similar
bequeathments inspired many acts of relief and on them are founded our
own charitable institutions. Even as early as 1549 a directive of
Edward the Sixth printed in his Prayer Book decreed that each church
display a poor box . . . "So many as are disposed shall offer to the
poorman's box everyone according to his ability and charitable mind".
Earliest charity item at March was entered in 1546:

- Item received of William Norman for the bequest of Henry Lambord,
  Upwell, 6s. 8d.
- 1550 - Payd to Browne for v yards of cloth to geve a pore woman,
  5s. 4d.
  - Paid for a shirt to wynde him in, 2s. 4d. (burial, no name)

The manufacture of paupers shirts and other items of clothing was
supervised by the churchwardens. Garments were allocated to the March
poor on the strength of the poor box:

- 1553 - Item for a payer of schoes for marget smarsoit, 10d.
  - Item for the lining of Wm. Cawthorne's coat, 1s. 6d.
  - Item for the said William's shirt making, 1d.
- 1560 - Item pd to William Mobb of ye Sweit Bryer for his seuts, 5s.

Some garments were made for March poor by tailors living at other
towns:

- 1594 - Item paid to Christopher Ellington and Nicholas Johnson for
  carrying the taylour to Spalding, 5s. 0d.

Monies accumulated in the town's poor box were not always for the
exclusive use of March poor. Indigent persons who wandered about seek-
ing a master relied in the meantime upon parish funds. There was no
welfare state as we understand it but each parish did its best to assist
the poor. As always, good ideals are open to abusement and it was soon
apparent that the swollen ranks of genuinely distressed people were
being infiltrated by vagrants who by their appearance were indisting-
uishable from deserving cases. Even church ministers and former monks
suffered the indignity of resorting to begging bowls. A former vicar
presented himself to the churchwarden in 1601 and was given a shilling.
Another recipient was a "gathering man" who had lost his belongings in
the West Country. He went away from March with 5s. in his purse.

Another poor man calling at March told of his having been a prisoner on
the high seas and received 1s. 6d. A beggar bearing the King's broad
seal, usually a mark of having served in a military capacity, was given
the same amount. One day an Irishman with his seven children came to
March; the churchwarden put a shilling in his bag. In the same year a
church minister turned up and for his miserable condition was given
2s. 6d. James Dighton, a local man, in 1643 lost his pig and was com-
pensated to the tune of 5s. A traveller robbed in 1653 received 6d. by
the churchwarden. Sixpence was also given to a soldier who had been a
prisoner in Holland. Two lame men discharged from hospital in 1654 had
no choice but to beg, and were given a special brief - the official
right to do so. They each received 6d. from the poor box. The list is
endless.

Aid went to children boarded out of town:

1577 - Pd to mother Armour for keeping of William Southold, 8s.
     - And for a yard of black freze for him, 6d.
     - And a quarter of white cloth to mend his hose, 4d.

In 1587 the poor box was the poorer by £1 "for keepyng of Lacey's
boy for a year" and "for putting forth of Barrett an almes childe,
10s." Paupers received burial on the parish, "Bunting's boy" committed
to the earth on the cheap - a mere 6d. The churchwardens of March
were approached by hundreds of distressed people, and they sometimes
dealt with petitions inviting parishioners to contribute to the relief
of people overtaken by disasters:

1707 - June 8: Collected upon a brief for loss by fire at Spilsby,
        18s. 0d. (£5,984 loss).
1707 - July 27: Collected upon a brief for ye repairing of Brosely
        Church, Salop, 13s. 6d. (Damage £1,390).
1707 - Aug. 10: Collected upon a brief for the loss by fire at
        Tow - cester, Northants, 15s. 3½d.
        June 31: Received of James Shepherd and Nicholas Cooledge,
        churchwardens for the town of March the sum of £1 19s. 10d.
        for money gathered upon a letter of request for a fire which
        happened in the town of Warboys. By me, Robert Poulter.

Entries referring to loss by fire relate mainly to house damage and
total destruction. Most residences were thatched and some attached.
March suffered from an outbreak of fire in 1666 - the year of the great
fire of London. Six houses were damaged or destroyed and payment made
to the occupiers:

1666 - April 7: Monney pde to the poor people wh was gathered upon
        the briefs what was gathered for the fire: Imprimis Pd to
        Thomas Mason 8s. 6d., Pd to Rchd Dawson 8s. 6d., Pd to Rob
        Burrows 8s. 6d., Pd to Widd Randall 6s. 6d., Pd to Widd
        Rawlings 6s. 6d., Pd to the Widd Sergeant 6s. 6d.

CHAPTER IX

Parish Officials

E have learned of the work of the CHURCHWARDEN. This officer was much involved with worldly matters and might be likened to a parish councillor. Churchwardens usually held office for a year, but there were odd exceptions. John Fage of March shared the position with various colleagues from 1543 to 1550. Edmund Conye and Roberde Coward of Whetylende (West End) held office from 1555 to 1560, handing over the office to Robert Conye and Thomas Bolland. These men supervised the town's earliest inventory compiled in the year of the Armada, 1586:

"Remaynynge unto Robert Conye and Thomas Bollard as followeth: Item. ij collars for bells, 4 iron hooks, ij goodyng (gudgeons), and ij old shears for bells, one weebe of lead, ij leaden brasses, ij old claspes, a lyttle bell and a ball of a bell clapper, iiij peces of lead solder, iij peces of bell metal, a communion booke, both the grants of our church, the deed of our tounehouse graunted us of the letter paten, and one other deed by the feofers of the same house . . . " (The grants were the Indulgence of Pope Clement vi, 1346, signed at Avignon, France (there were two Popes at the time!), and the Indulgence of Cardinal Wolsey, 1526.

Churchwardens collected rates and looked after the town's indigent poor. They attended the Bishop's Council, purchased armour and weapons and furniture, silver plate and communion books. They superintended all public works and attended to the needs of the Constables, Surveyor and Fenreves (the latter held rights of common). The churchwarden received no payment but was allowed expenses. They were not always trustworthy! Mr. Prance had been elected to the office and a remarkable entry was made concerning him:

1647 - Paid Wm. Tayler for watching Mr. Prance his home, 1s.
       - Paid to Edmond Simpson for the lyke, 1s.

The matter also involved the other churchwarden, Mr. Saul. It is strange that this man was considered a suitable candidate, as he had earlier been presented for non-payment of rates. Obviously the two men connived, but the town Constables flushed them out:

1647 - Paid to Mr. Barret for moveing the Judge to Ely assises
       for an order to bringe John Saul to an account for
       embeslinge the town stock.

Churchwardens dealt with all manner of problems, such as going to Manea in 1561 to view the commons over a boundary dispute, and to Whittlesey "to help lay out the fens" (another boundary matter). In

1610 they were responsible for the removal of two vagrants from Cambridge to Wisbech, and in 1613 the churchwardens obtained a book for the parish, entitled "Mr. Jewell's Works" (author of "Judicious Hooker").

Allied to the churchwardens responsibilities the office of SURVEYOR OF THE HIGHWAY is traceable to 1546. The Surveyor was responsible for roads and bridges, a daunting task in the Fens. Many of the roads were submerged in winter and incurred a great deal of expense. The Surveyor was responsible for driving new roads for improved access to working areas, as in the case of Burrowmoor Road:

> Delivered to hands of Roberd Rowlinson for the makyng (in 1546) of a waye into Borow more, xis. The xxxviij yer of our soverayn lord Kynge Henry the viiit.

These few extracts from the churchwardens' book give some idea of the Surveyor's task:

> 1560 – Item paid to William Acard for rowing Brods horse to Well, 1s.
> – Item paid to William Reynold for rowing to Ely, 1s.
> 1595 – Paid to Christopher Ellington for rowing John Lewis to Wysbech, 1s. 1d.
> 1606 – Surveyors of the ways have 35s. entrusted to them to lay out.
> 1623 – Money expended upon the highways, £3 11s. 9d.
> 1666 – For my horse to London and Surrey, 16s.

March was saddled with a heavy burden in keeping the bridge along Aldreth Causeway in good repair. Other parishes were responsible for easier stretches of the Causeway, usually about 20 poles each. March had rather more to look after – 30 poles including the leam bridge with its deteriorating heads and coffers. In the 16th century the annual expenditure for this amounted to 7s. March also maintained Stutbridge, Goolebridge and Lanthorn bridge as well as the Nene bridge. This was a very considerable outlay of money and a hard worked Surveyor!

The town bore the total cost of repair to its own pavements:

> 1543 – Delivered by the goode wyfe Estmonde accounte, the dyscharge of Thomas Estmonde last wyfe for the payment of the repracyonz of the caussys the som of vli. (Thomas Estmonde's second wife and widow gave £5 towards the repair of March roads. Monies to repair roads were sometimes bequeathed).

The CONSTABLE'S main duty was to take note and observe strangers to the town. He interviewed them and examined letters or briefs in their possession. If he was dissatisfied he simply escorted them to the parish boundary and instructed them to be on their way. If they did anything wrong they were apprehended, taken to the town magistrate, ordered away, placed in gaol or whipped:

> 1614 – More allowed Reynold Walsham for whipping John Graver being taken as a vagabond, vid.

1620 - Pd for carrying of Jeff Rogers to the gaol, xiid.

Several items refer to the collecting of monies by Constables from parishioners "for the prisoners at Ely" and building there. They also cared for the town armour. In 1620 the Constable removed from the town a character called Wynlove and his "idle, noisy friends" from a March house. This bunch was placed in a boat and rowed by the Constable to Outwell. Blind beggars were not tolerated at March. They were considered a liability on the parish and the Constable escorted them to the boundary and gave them a direction to a distant town. When "sertain gipsies" encamped near March in 1622 the Constables spent a few uncomfortable nights in a concealed place, watching them. The following accounts are typical of the Constable's lot (Recorded in 1623):

For three hues and cries, 1s. 6d.
To a wench that went to Over, 2d.
For the arming of three town pickets, 3s. (A cause for alarm).
For a hue and cry sent to Wisbech, 4d. (Those Wisbech men!)
For a vagrant sent to Murrow, 10d.

The policy was to turn undesirable people away - even if it meant giving them a few pence. Other parishes did the same thing, so the poor wretches knew no home - just the open road.

1659 - Given to Sergeant to send him out of town, 8s.
1665 - Item paid for a warrant for the blind piper, 1s. 6d.
   - Item spent in going to Wisbech to complain of one Bowell
     and his wife, 1s. 6d. (That Wisbech- March feud!)
   - Spent in following Mouse and Leary with the Constables, 6d.
1666 - Paid to John Ingram for a pannell and baskets to carry
   Amy Persons children.
1675 - Spent when the tobacker pipe maker lay in bond (gaol), 8d.
   - Spent when the thick legged tailor lay in bond, 8d.

The PARISH CLERK-CUM-SEXTON was a busy man, too. Before the Reformation he served as Holy Water Bearer and generally made an ideal candidate for Holy Orders. The Clerk kept' the church tidy and undertook house-to-house sprinkling with holy water. This was the most rewarding part of his duties as it was customary for householders to give him a present. Linked to the Clerk's post was that of BELLMAN, the product of the late mediaeval era. He was initially employed to ring funeral knells, a lucrative position. Bellmen carried handbells and in so doing were the forerunners of the Town Crier. The ringing of handbells proclaimed obituaries and masses of the next day, reminding guild members of their obligations.

Earliest entry of a Clerk at St. Wendreda's church was made in 1542. When he acted as Sexton he regularly swept the steeple stairway - more than eighty steps - an uncomfortable, dusty and draughty job as the writer well knows. The Sexton took his brush to the treasure house and occasionally helped the priest to prepare wax and make candles. One of the old-time Sexton's, Mr. Wylkynson, swept the church dutifully and strewed it with straw and reed, a job which was later allocated to the Bellman.

A Bellman was first appointed to St. Wendreda's church in 1560. He did other jobs in the town, but chimed the bells in a part-time capacity. The usual annual remuneration was 8s. 6d., but Wylkynson received 10s. His tools of trade was a spade and shovel which implied that he not only rang the corpse to the church, he also buried it. Mr. Wylkynson was succeeded by Mr. Seix or Sexe and this man gave stirling service to the church and town for at least 30 years.

1571 - Payd to Seix for three days' work, xviijd.

1574 - Payd to Ambrose Sexe for strawynge ye church agaynst Whit Sunday, vid.

Another Bellman, affectionately known as "father fricke", sometimes helped the Sexton. His favourite job was to make sure the surplices were clean and smart for the services. When Father Fricke had died, we read of a Mr. Johnsonne acting as Bellman. At the same time Michael West was appointed Sexton. The latter was a very practical man and glazed windows and cleaned the leads, felled thorns and maintained the churchyard in addition to church duties. It was he who crept into the church one day, climbed the steps to the ringing gallery armed with a blunderbus and commenced to slaughter bats and pigeons that had gathered in the roof.

1598 - Paid for showtin sartin showth (shot) at varmin about the church, vid.
(This accounts for lead shot taken from the angel roof).

West was succeeded by John Thompson, and he was promptly given an extra job - that of sweeping the streets. He assisted in beating the bounds for the procession (establishing boundary rights). Before the processions started the Sexton had to fill in pot-holes in the road.

Last but not least, the PRIEST at March was really a curate-in-charge, being directly responsible to the Bishop. After ecclesiastical authority at Doddington had ceased, the Manor or Palace there was sold to the Crown on June 10th, 1600. Queen Elizabeth I held it for one year and then sold the property for £300 and an annual payment of £74 to Sir John Peyton. Rectors continued at Doddington and they appointed curates to March until circa 1870.

The earliest recorded curate at March, Syr Thomas Wryght, is seen under the year 1517. He was succeeded by Syr Wylliam Metcalfe. Curates did not sojourn long in the town. Apart from their normal church duties, they presided over vestry meetings and visited parishioners and comforted sick and dying persons. They held no authority in administering the dues and demands of the town. A few acted as schoolmasters in order to embellish their meagre stipend. A building, known as The Nunnery, near the church, accommodated the curates and their families until later they removed to High Street.

The curate wrote letters and witnessed documents and wills; he assumed responsibility for the church registers and allocated seats in church.

Memorandum: It is agreed by common consent of the curate and churchwardens and two of the best of every wardship shall between this and Whitsunday next place the parishioners in decent and good order.

The registers were also signed by the curate, and he ordered paper for the same:

"For two quers of papper to make a register booke".

To help him the curate appointed a SCRIBE, who probably worked on a part-time basis in the town's treasure house. He began his labours thus:

"The Regester Booke of Marche, all the christenynge, burynge and marriage beginning at the 25 day of Marche, Anno Dom 1558 one year after another as followeth!"

The good scribe, Martin, conscientiously and patiently recorded 30 years of entries into his new volume and had it signed by the curate. The writer of this present work records his grateful acknowledgement to that worthy man of four hundred years ago for his diligence without which this history of March would not have materialised. His successors too made a valuable contribution.

Occasionally visiting clergy preached in the church and were paid for their participation.

1614 - Given to Mr. Robinson preacher for his sermon, 5s. 4d.
1619 - Given to the blind man for preaching, 6s. 8d.

The Civil War made its inevitable contribution in the quality and allocation of preachers. Mr. Trigg, curate, saw the High Sheriff about the notorious ship-rate, hoping to get a reduction for the town. The curate often received presents for representing the inhabitants in times of difficulty:

1639 - Paid for a book and a hood and cap for the minister £2 0s. 6d

During the Commonwealth the curate had to give way to approved Puritan ministers, like the Ironsides, well drilled in idealistic concepts, as was the mood of the powerful Republic. They were met with more than a little scepticism.

1655 - Expended to Tho. Neale for the dinner of the gentleman that came to preach at the final lecture.
(The lectures were really a form of brain washing!)
Many clergy and curates were deemed unworthy. Cromwell harrassed them, but credit to him he would not suffer unsuitable clerics. Many meetings took place in order to distinguish good clergy from the bad.

1655 - Layd out for goeing to Cambridge about scandulous and insufficient ministers, 10s.

Finally, a word about the BAILIFF. This man looked for trouble! He was not involved with direct administration but his post was very necessary. As early as the 14th century he was appointed to enforce laws regulating the standard of manufacture and the sale of bread and beer. Most brewers were women, a kind of part-time occupation while their husbands worked on the commons or at the fisheries. The women were not always careful about the quality of their pints! A report of 1397 indicates that the ladies of Mercheford were familiar with sharp practice:

"MERCHEFORD - The examiners of beer there report that Agnes Spynk, Clera Webster, Agnes Wells, Margaret Hockery and Isabella Worm are brewers of beer and have sold contrary to the assize". Isabella was fined 2d. and her colleagues 6d. each. "John Conellyn and Thomas Wilson are the examiners and have not done their duty". Fined 3d. "Katheryn Ray, Dulcie Wynt, Alice Haldyn, Anna Lyghthope, Colletta Cooper are brewers of beer and have sold contrary to the assize". Fined 3d., 8d., 4d., 6d. and 4d. respectively. "And Alice Cleylon and Agnes Presson are beer sellers who have broken the assize". Similarly fined. "Jon Baxter bakes bread white and good but has broken the assize". Fined 8d. "Agnes Winge and Beatrice Hert are bakers and have broken the assize". Fined 2d. each. "John Russell and John Bole are the examiners and have not done their duty". Fined 3d. each.

The men who had not done their duty of reporting improper practice, such as short measure, etc., surely had free pints to the point of overflowing! The women were cleverly corrupting the bailiff's assistants in return, it is assumed, for a blind eye! There is no chance nowadays of achieving the same effect. March pubs have pretty ladies serving behind the bars, but the stuff they hand over is brewed miles away.

The George, High Street, March; much restored

St. Mary's Church, March

An early 17th century residence, West End, March

A pantiled cottage of c. 1830, Elwyn Road, March

Georgian houses, High Street, March

Modern cottages given the old treatment, West End, March

CHAPTER X

Population versus Plague

FROM the seventh century to circa 1100 the number of people living at the hamlet of Merche can be reckoned at between 50 and 100. Merche was an outlying settlement of Doddington and the majority of the island's population was centred on the mother village. The 13th century witnessed a gradual increase in the settlements and Merche and Mercheford began to outstrip its parent, something in the region of 300 and 400 living along the riverside and about 200 housed in the original settlement in the vicinity of the church.

A major contributory factor and an obstacle in the development of communities was plague and pestilence. Thirteen-forty-seven witnessed the terrible decimation of the country's population due to that dreaded visitation, Bubonic plague - the Black Death introduced by the rat flea. At about that time, while there were sufficient builders around, the chancel arch and the south doorway of St. Wendreda's church were built. Generally the Fens did not suffer excessively from the plague as few visitors entered the area. A great deal of ecclesiastical business did however take place at Ely and Peterborough and those places suffered. At Ely a whole street was wiped out and at Wisbech with its port, suffering occurred there, the lord of the manor making over a large area of land to accommodate the bodies of people struck down by the plague. Many years later when it was all over monuments sprang up all over the land, some in memory of those that perished and some as a thanksgiving of deliverance. Several flat topped towers such as that of St. Wendreda's church, erected circa 1380 were later capped with spires, beheld by the inhabitants as a finger pointing to heaven, praising God for His abundant mercies.

Depopulation of the country was profoundly evident in the century following the Black Death in which time nearly all building activities ceased. It was not until the reign of Queen Elizabeth I, 200 years later, that the birth rate made up the population levels existing prior to 1340. A measuring rod can be applied to March between 1560 and 1570, that decade introducing 334 live births and 200 deaths - an addition over the period of 134 to a population (1560) of about 850. In 1600 March began to expand into the commons and there were upwards of 200 houses in the town. Allowing for an average of five people per house, we may assume that there were 1,000 people living here. Plague was spasmodic, occurring here and there sometimes in small doses, and at other times in terrifying proportions. Between 1600 and 1625 383 baptisms were recorded at March as against 634 burials. This was a bad time.

From 1625 to 1650, 960 babes were lovingly borne to the Norman font for baptism. The town bier carried 793 coffins over the same period. There was not a significant increase in the population. At the Restoration in 1660 the population of March stood at 1,200 and from then on there was a steady increase, albeit the odd plague. The register of 1638 tells of an unusually large increase in deaths. There was an average number from January to July (10), but when harvesting operations were at their peak the mortality rate increased alarmingly. In August that year, seven sad processions approached the church, followed by eight in September and eleven in October. Twelve burials took place in both November and December and in the following January and February the sexton had prepared 26 new graves. From Lady Day to Lady Day March had suffered no less than 90 deaths from a population of just over a thousand. This was mainly due to outbreaks of plague and it is known that whole families were wiped out. The Adams first lost mother Jone. She was followed by Mary and Katherine, daughters, and finally her husband was laid beside her. Two Neale girls succumbed to the "pest" and a little while later their father, William, was carried to the grave. John Shepherd lost five members of his family that year. Hugh Vicker listened to the mournful knell for his son and two daughters.

In 1681 March had a population of about 1,600 and there was every indication that expansion to an appreciable extent was beginning. The fenreves with their rights of common were happy to graze their stock on those considerable acres but they did not desire that townspeople build on the commons with which the town was practically surrounded. This was a problem for young couples and some – desperate for a place to build upon, moved onto the commons. The fenreves were lenient however, and imposed small fines but allowed people to stay. Most houses were built of lath and plaster, bricks being very expensive. A kiln in March was owned by Maximilian Walsham, his bricks selling at 20s. per hundred. Thatch was 15s. for 600 of reed, the thatcher receiving 17s. 6d. for seven days thatching. Labourers received less than a shilling a day, and one man, Roman Quince, took home 11s. 8d. for 14 days of hedging. Throughout the 18th century, the town's population appeared to be more stable and at the beginning of the 19th century stood at about 2,514. In 1831 it had increased to 5,147 and 10 years later had reached 5,706. In 1849 approximately 6,300 people lived at March.

That was an innoble year for the town. It experienced its worst mortality rate ever. Indeed March was said for its size to have the worst death rate in the whole of the country. The severe outbreak of various diseases at March was a repetition of that which occurred in 1832, only much worse. There were in 1849 1,215 dwellings in the town, the majority along the riverside, along High Street and in the Little London area. Many of them were little more than hovels with shared toilets usually situated above foul drains. The town had 986 paupers while the remainder of North Witchford did not exceed 1,100. Pauper homes were lamentable. Those unfortunate people could not afford to eat properly and there were severe cases of undernourishment and malnutrition. They were assailed by the ague, typhoid, cholera and diarrhoea, these accounting for most deaths, amounting to no less than 441 in the space of 12 months. Mumps, bronchitis and atrophy added their measure, too.

The Report from the Board of Health was embarrassingly revealing. In those days March had the reputation of being a township of brothels and beer houses, but the same could be said for other towns. These dubious attractions were partly attributable to large numbers of strangers coming to the Fens to seek work on the land. The main problems were the River Nene and an old waterway called The Hythe which ran along the west side of High Street towards the Avenue. They were little more than open sewers. Many residences had cess pits sunk within a few feet of wells, the water of which was used for drinking and other purposes. One well was situated near a cemetery. The most contagious areas in March were Little London (present car park site), the Sumps, the rear of the King William, White Pump, High Dyke, Bellmetal Lane, Shearhod's Row, Millyard, Lambs Yard, Well-end (Nene Parade), Norwoodside, Lewin's Yard, Bond's Yard and Tait's Yard. Contents from slaughter houses were thrown into an open ditch and the town had numerous pigsties and open privies. Some houses had low ceilings beneath which one could not stand and no windows, and sleeping as many as eight or more people to a room. Hygiene was unheard of.

The Government inspector reported that Little London was the worst seat of disease. "Everything that can tend to lower health and destroy lives of the inhabitants is to be found there in its most aggravated form'.' There were a large number of lodging homes in the town, said to be unhealthy and calculated to inflict serious injury upon the community. Some of these places were almost surrounded by foul, stagnant ditches.

Despite this grave setback, after March had been "cleansed" and piped water provided the community began to expand into the shape and size with which we are familiar. March overtook Whittlesey, Chatteris and Ely mainly because of the establishment of the railway centre. By 1911 March had a population of 8,403 and in 1931 11,266 - a thousand fewer than Wisbech. The population of March in 1951 is recorded at 12,993 and at the time of writing (1984) stands at approximately 14,700.

Late 15th century Double Hammer-beam Angel Roof   Reputedly the finest example in England

Mechanics' Institute Broad Street

The First 'Centenary' Baptist Building 1799

Bridge area, March, circa 1912

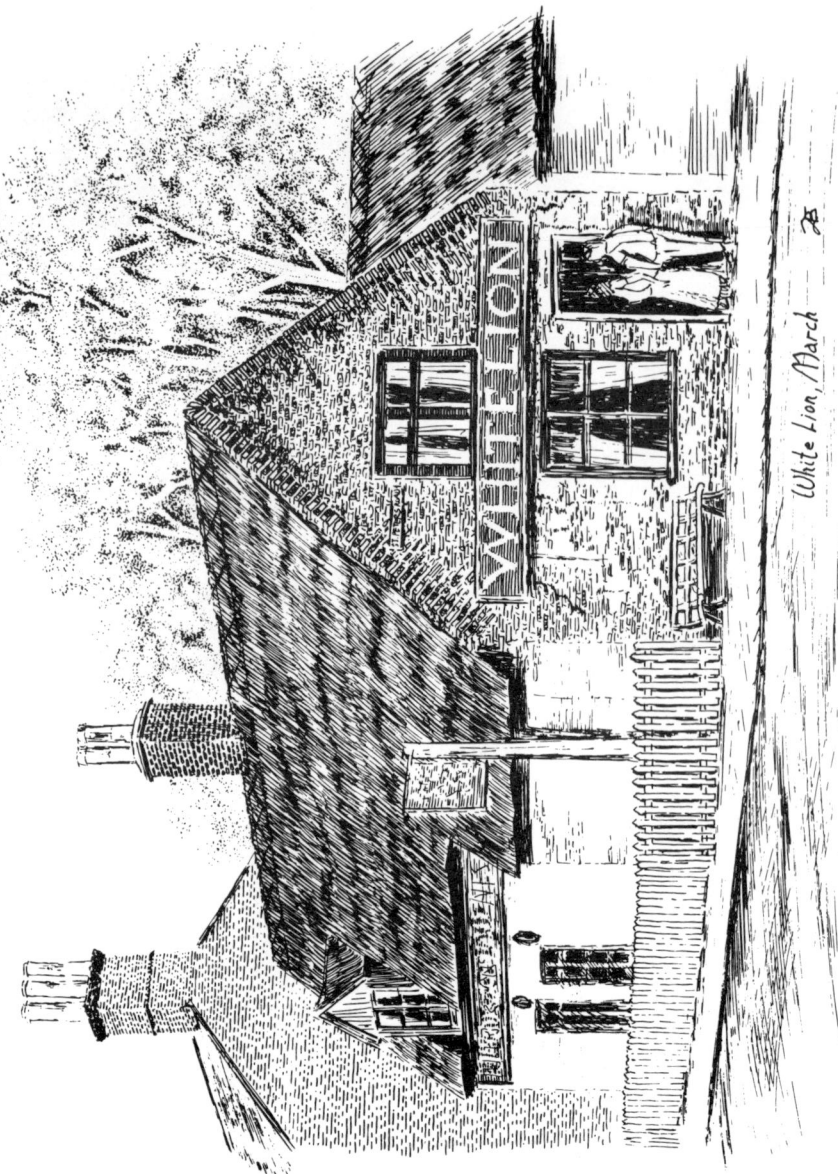

White Lion, March

The Beeches, High Street

The White Hart, circa 1905

Bevis

River Nene, March c. 1900

Town End Corner, March

Dartford Road, c 1890

The Old Mill, Burrowmoor Road

Riverside Cottages, March

Church Street, March : Cottage on left bore date 1658

CHAPTER XI

The Past Three Centuries

BEFORE 1680 the Fenland economy was based on fish, fowl, beast, sheep, osiers and reeds. Little had changed in a thousand years. The inhabitants, sometimes called Beezlings and Girvii seldom ventured onto the uplands and the upland men were not inclined to enter the Fens – except on business. Fish and fowl from the Fens were very popular in city markets, including London, and Fen horses, recognised for strength and stamina were bred for the army. Reeds sold well to people of the upland areas. Wheat was grown on the Fen islands and certain other crops did well on soil subjected to winter inundation. The men of March found gainful employment at the fisheries and wildfowling was a lucrative business there being many decoys in which birds were trapped, in the locality. The commons were ideal for grazing herds and flocks, and boars and sows grew fat on beechnuts. Thousands of wild duck were slaughtered by the murderous blast of the punt gun, the 7ft. barrel aimed along the bottom of the punt and capable of killing upwards of 12 dozen birds with a single discharge of lead shot. One man, Bury by name, working on Whittlesey Mere is said to have killed 36 dozen with one shot! The Fenman was not as a general rule too sociable with visitors, seemed contented with his lot, minded his own business and thanked no-one to interfere with his life style. Heaven help anyone who did.

Interfering "foreigners" had other ideas! It had long been visualised that if the vast Fen level were drained, the peat and silt soil would transform the area into the richest agricultural plain in England. As early as the 13th century monks at Thorney had pioneered a modest drainage scheme near the abbey and on the site of former marsh grew all kinds of things with creditable success. Between then and the mid 17th century only a few half hearted attempts transpired to drain parts of the fen. In the fourth decade of the century the Earl of Bedford and a committee of gentlemen adventurers, with the King's blessing, set out to rid the Fens of water once and for all. This prodigous undertaking was supervised by the eminent Dutch drainage engineer, Cornelius Vermuyden. Experiencing great difficulty in employing English workmen, Vermuyden brought in willing foreigners to help him achieve his designs. Hundreds of Dutch and Scottish prisoners of war from battles of the Civil War, were drafted into the Fens to cut out and embank miles of drains and dykes, helped and supervised by Huguenot and Walloon refugees who had fled to England in order to escape religious persecution. They introduced new techniques of manufacturing linen and other cloth, but the Walloons in particular were highly skilled land drainage workers and when they had finished the drainage work many turned their hands to farming. Not a few foreign names are to be found in the Fens to this day, descendants of those industrious Scots, Dutch and Huguenot and Walloon refugees.

Fenmen were averse to foreigners and disputed the plans verbally and with physical action whenever opportunity arose. It was abundantly clear that the eventual drainage of the area would in the short term deprive them of a living. Many became redundant and the Fenland was overtaken with a severe depression. This further added to the problem of the normal influx of masterless men, still reeling from the effects of the Dissolution a century before. Numerous briefs were read out in the churches in aid of dispossessed families. Gradually more and more land was brought under the plough, and farmers with an eye to the future, visualised correctly the hidden potential of thousands of acres of marsh then in the process of being drained. Hundreds of acres of marsh were purchased. Large houses were built in March and other Fen towns, many displaying the opulence of the Georgian and early Victorian eras.

Although the area suffered from depression, this transitional stage led to a bright new dawn as far as Fenland economy was concerned. Boats, nets, eel-traps and fish spears which had meant so much in financial terms were swept away and replaced with spades, hoes, harrows and ploughshares. The wind engines and later steam engines drew the water along miles of watercourses, depositing it into tidal rivers and a new and virile land emerged. From the former watery wilderness the promise became reality and the Fens with good reason were called The Larder of England. The land was so light that at first it was unnecessary to plough it. Rollers were constantly used. Young crops grew so vigorously that it was necessary to employ women and children to trample them into the ground in order to delay them. Some crops grew successfully with as much as a farrow. Crops thriving on old reed beds assumed in full measure the profits of systematic cultivation and at last the spectre of unemployment receded.

Even despite the rapidly developing Fenland economy, March land workers looked enviously at their colleagues at Thorney. The workforce there was employed by the Duke of Bedford on his 17,000 acre estate. They lived in fine cottages with water laid on and bathrooms. It was nothing like that at March. It was many years before the men of March benefited to such extent socially and culturally as did the men of Thorney who had a library, lecture hall and educational facilities at their disposal. When the time for March to benefit had arrived, it came in the smell of grease, smoke and steam. As the flesh horse had made its mark on March over the centuries, now the hour of the iron horse had come. Steam was at the heart of the industrial revolution at March and the town became the envy of larger places in East Anglia. The railway engine brought among many things, stability and increase of March populations and a new Fenman appeared in the shape of the smartly attired, well-paid, elite class of worker - the footplate man.

Largely thanks to the shortsightedness of Wisbech banker and Quaker Lord Peckover, March was fortunate to have the rail centre develop on its very own doorstep. At the outset the railway company desired to establish the centre at Wisbech and Lord Peckover agreed to sell land to this purpose. But he imposed an insufferable condition upon the Company: that the railway would not work on Sundays. March accepted the railway centre - but only just. Influential farmers were opposed to the railway as they believed it would attract men from the land. As it was the railway did not detract seriously from agricultural enterprise. March had suffered a 12 per cent decrease in its population and the Town Council had no choice but to wave the green flag to the railway company. The advent of steam freight at March and the establishment of the famous Whitemoor marshalling yards considerably enhanced the town's image and a minor boom was the result. Because of March's centralised position and convenient rail access it received the coveted title of County Town. Here was built County Hall which to this day is still an important administrative centre under the new title of Fenland Hall. However March did not take advantage of the railway. Little industry was attracted to the town and it must be said that March was in an eminently good position for this with its huge railway sidings to hand. It was left to Wisbech to surge ahead with its industrial enterprise, especially that centred on the canning industry.

THE TOWN EXPANDS

March is fortunate in possessing a number of well-built 19th century houses and cottages. An appreciable number of earlier houses survive dating from the 1620's to 1800. It was a pity that the old cottages known as The Long Eight in The Causeway were pulled down. They were built in circa 1825 from materials purchased at the site of Norman Cross prisoner-of-war camp, Yaxley. The camp was purpose built to accommodate many thousands of soldiers captured in the Napoleonic Wars. Several houses and cottages along West End and Nene Parade were rebuilt in the 19th century. A few older premises like that near the Health Centre and one with Dutch gables further along the riverside, were fortunately untouched. The first mentioned has exceptionally fine beams as does The Ship in Nene Parade. The White Horse and The Ship date back to the 17th century, the former with later additions. The George is another old inn, but much restored. The Ship may not always have been a public house but it once had a "dungeon" in which drunks were cast to cool off! Fine Georgian buildings can be seen along High Street and near the Market Place the Griffin Hotel can be traced back to the 1630's and it is thought to date back to Tudor times. Another old pub is the Red Lion and The Acre near the Park is believed to have been built between 1830 and 1850. It was known as The Acre Inn and was the popular haunt of bargees and their families. The Horse and Jockey is another "oldie" but several charming old pubs in March were recently demolished.

The White Hart building still stands near the bridge; no longer is it
an inn but serves as offices. The Bull, The Carpenters Arms, The
Wheel, The Windmill, The Robin Hood, The White Lion and others - all
have gone. For the record there is still The Lord Nelson, The Northern,
Wades Hotel, Temperence Hotel, Coachmakers Arms, George and Star, Royal
Exchange, The Cock, King William, Seven Stars, Rose and Crown, Hammer
and Anvil, Jack of Trumps and the latest The Men of March.

The market at March is a fairly extensive one. At one time it consisted of 14 covered stalls but it did not enjoy success. Nearby stood
the Butter Cross - an obelisk - which was removed before 1900. The stocks
were sited here and in them was placed a variety of offenders, among
them people who objected going to church. The Fire Station was sited on
the Market Place, the building preceding the present Law Courts -
formerly the Town Hall - having an ancient clock now kept in the tower
of St. Peter's church. In the last century the Fire Brigade was hastily
summoned by the ringing of a small bell known as the "Ting-tang".
Horses hauling council refuse carts were detached and made to gallop
through the streets to the market place to be hitched to the engine.

Several warehouses stood on the riverside to facilitate river trade.
From the 16th century March had a minor port with connections with other
small Fenland ports and the larger port of Wisbech. Considerable quan-
tities of corn, coal and timber passed through March, some unloaded onto
the Acre Wharf next to the Steam Mills, the buildings surviving well
into the 20th century. A large granary nearby was regularly topped up
with grain unloaded from the barges which were turned round in a
u-shaped loop just off the river. Owned by Owen Gray, Esq., the
granary was at one time used as a theatre. After the theatre proprietor
- a Mr. Smedley - had built a new theatre, the town's Independents used
the granary for religious services. The granary was purchased by John
Smith in 1840 and he erected the mill and installed a new steam engine.
This was a beneficial enterprise to March.

The curates of March resided in a Georgian house in High Street.
They enjoyed the surrounds of $1\frac{1}{2}$ acres of exotic gardens planted with
American plants and evergreens, etc. They were patronised by visitors
travelling long distances to see them. In 1830 there were no less than
11 schools at March. One was held in the existing winged building in
High Street then the Guild Hall built in 1827. The school was run by
the National System; the headmaster received £100, and the school-
mistress £50 annually. The town's oldest educational institution,
the former March Grammar School came into being at the end of the 17th
century. It was absorbed together with the town's Secondary Schools
into the present Comprehensive system. In 1830 the majority of March
schools were held at private residences situated in Whittle-end, High
Street, Well-end, Stone Cross and Town End. Adults availed themselves
of educational opportunities provided in the Mechanics Institute. This
was formerly a theatre standing on the site of the Nat-West bank.

Founded on October 3rd, 1845, the Institute had three rooms - reading, lecture and for the use of committees. When occasion necessitated these could be converted into one large room. The Mechanics' Institute was of great benefit to members of the working class and promoted useful and general knowledge. It had a museum and a library.

TRANSPORT - 19th century style

A hundred and fifty years ago transport in the Fens was undertaken with difficulty. Roads were deplorable, deeply pitted and furrowed. Some were annually ploughed over by farmers to restore some kind of evenness. Waterways provided alternative routes to other parishes and the rivers were well used by passenger boats. A passenger/luggage boat service was run by John Smith in the first half of the 19th century. He plied between Cambridge and March once a fortnight and once a week to King's Lynn. Day and Co's wagon departed from the White Hart on Mondays and Thursdays at 6 a.m. enroute to St. Ives, Cambridge and London. Gilby and Wallis's wagon left the Chequers every Wednesday and Saturday evening to the same destination. Brighton's cart left the White Lion for Downham Market on Wednesdays. John Robert's cart went to Whittlesey from the White Hart on Mondays and Fridays, and Day and Co. ran a cart from the White Hart on Mondays and Fridays to Wisbech.

The "Day" and the "Defiance" made a splash of colour in town dashing away from The Griffin Inn to London via Cambridge, Wades Mill and Ware. Between them the coaches covered the week and surely evoked much interest among the townspeople as, adorned in smart livery, they reined in at the Griffin where the reinsman and his guard climbed down and relaxed with tankards of ale to regale them.

Local traders valued the custom of the gentry. The poorer classes purchased items of necessity, but ladies and gentlemen of means enjoyed plentiful luxuries in the way of food and clothes. In the 19th century their extra spending habits played an important role in the stability of the local economy and the gentlefolk were well pleased to see their names published in various directories. Many of the old trades are no more: basket makers, sieve makers, boot and shoe makers, straw hat makers, tallow chandlers, whitesmiths, fellmongers, brassfounders, stay makers, braziers, gilders . . . to mention a few, all had their businesses at March.

Many items were made to order such as boots and shoes, hats and gloves. Mass manufacturing was then unheard of and would not be until higher wages were obtained. Local manufacturers were their own retailers and some private premises combined factory and shop. It was largely due to the industrial revolution, epitomised by the cogwheel that the old crafts began to die. We have a similar situation in the ascendancy of micro-chips which have brought into being a new race of masterless men. History does repeat itself. The old, valued crafts, few indeed nowadays teach us of the truth of good quality and simplicity.

March of 150 years ago had a large number of professional and commercial premises: of these 111 were in High Street, Well End had 20, Bridge Street (Broad Street) 20, Whittle End 18, Market Place 6, Sumps 6, Town End 6, Stone Cross 2, Bellmetal Lane 1, Brooks Lane 1, Wisbech Road 1, Church End 1, Norwood 1, High Dyke 1 - Total 195.

In 1825 March had 10 building firms, 10 bakers, 6 blacksmiths, 8 boot and shoe makers, 4 brewers, 3 brickmakers, 8 butchers, 4 carpenters, 3 glass dealers, 3 chemists, 2 clothes dealers, 3 coopers, 5 coal and corn merchants, 7 fire and office agents, 3 attorneys, 3 auctioneers 3 fishmongers, 10 gardeners and seedsmen, 2 glovers, 8 grocers and drapers, 2 hairdressers, 2 ironmongers, 2 lime burners, 2 malsters, 4 millers, 7 dressmakers, 7 millwrights, 3 painters and plumbers, 2 ropemakers, 3 saddlers, 5 general shopkeepers, 5 straw hat makers, 3 surgeons, 4 surveyors, 10 tailors, 1 tallow chandler, 2 watch and clock makers, 5 wheelwrights and a bank (Gurneys, Birdbeck and Peckovers (branch of Wisbech Bank), Well End. In 1850 two additional Banks National Provincial Bank of England and Harvey and Hudson's had established business at March.

Before the end of the 19th century, March St. Wendreda's church was separated from Doddington Rectory and became a parish in its own right. Provision was made for three additional parishes to serve the town, recognising that the community was rapidly expanding. St. John's church was built in 1872, St. Mary's in 1873 and St. Peter's in 1881. The cemetery chapel in Station Road was erected about the same time as St. John's. Another church was later erected in Whittlesey Road and was under the supervision of the rector of St. Mary's; owing to the dearth of population in that area the church was closed down and eventually sold. It was demolished in recent years. March has a long testimony of nonconformity. A Baptist congregation assembled in 1672 and a Baptist church in High Street was first used in 1799. This was rebuilt as Centenary Baptist Church in 1870; after the First World War it was severely damaged by fire and rebuilt. A Strict Baptist congregation apparently existed at March in 1765, meeting at the home of Thomas Bowls. The minister was Samuel Fullilove who later removed to Benwick. The church seems to have been reorganised in 1821 by a Mr. Bevill who held services in his own house. Providence Strict Baptist church was built in 1849.

Congregationalists assembled in a granary before moving to their new church in Station Road in 1836. It is now the United Reformed Church. The Methodist cause first came to March in 1829. A fine church was erected in High Street about sixty years later. The Primitive Methodists established a church at March in 1848. The Roman Catholics worshipped in a uninspiring church in St. John's Road before moving a short distance to an impressive new church in the same road. A community of Sisters are based on that church. The Salvation Army came to March between 1900 and 1904 and meet in The Citadel in High Street.

The congregation of Jehovah's Witnesses built a church c. 1980 on the site of an old house (once used as a chapel) in Bevill's Yard. Before 1900 the Hon. Alexandra Peckover declared open a Railway Mission near March Station yard; it is disused.

The First World War had no marked effect upon Fenland towns in general. At March commercial life continued much as before, but practically every family knew the trauma of losing sons and fathers in the battles waged on the Continent. Several March men did not return as can be realised when scanning the names engraved on the town's memorial to the dead in Broad Street. At the time March was sustained from its agricultural position and the fact that almost every household kept a prolific garden. The railway was of immense importance and a great deal of traffic passed through. But it was not until the Second World War that the railway at March, then embodied in a complex marshalling yard, on Whitemoor came into its own, making a magnificent contribution to the war effort on a national scale. During the war several local women were employed at Whitemoor, starting work at 7.30 a.m. and ending their day at 5 p.m. Some were porters, some cleaned coaches and others cleaned and oiled points (there were 700 sets), weeded the permanent way and removed scrap. It was vital that the huge complex be maintained in first class order 24 hours of the day. It is difficult to emphasise the importance of the country's largest railway marshalling yard in the time of war when in the region of 400 trains were handled each day. Nowadays the yards resemble a ghost town - the result of economical measures.

The railway system at March was opened on August 20th, 1883. At the outbreak of World War II in 1939 Whitemoor marshalling yards were one of the largest in Europe. In 1884 the daily average of goods and passenger trains passing through March amounted to 310. By the 'twenties the rail facilities at March were entirely inadequate and the complex underwent expensive modernisation. Techical knowhow of German railway experts who had perfected electric retarding systems played a major role in the enlargement of Whitemoor. The Germans provided much of the material. The railway at March earned fame for its vital contribution towards victory, but when the war had ended the railway yards declined and with them the "Golden Rail". The elite worker - the footplate man and his prestige - was no more.

Many people living at March during the war did not realise that the railway yards contained awful destructive power in the form of truck loads of high explosive shells and bombs which were shunted away usually at night. It seems odd that the enemy made no attempt to destroy the yards. It has been said that this was because the enemy had hoped to use them. Certainly he was interested in Whitemoor for he dropped flares above it now and then in order to observe what was going on. Disruptive attacks were made on railway lines leading into March.

Between 1940 and 1944 there were 40 bombing incidents in March and district, this including the bombing of Norwood Road during which some residents lost their lives. In the same area 20 aircraft - British, American and German, crashed or crash landed and a flying bomb exploded on a farm not far from St. Wendreda's church. After the war masons cleaned the War Memorial displaying the names of 209 men of March who lost their lives in the Battle of the Somme and other foreign fields, and added a further 102 names of townspeople who, 21 years later had laid down their lives in the cause of freedom.

Modern March views the loss of its railway enterprise with understandable apprehension and disappointment. It was a mistake in not attempting to procure industry while the railway was able to offer first class facilities. That is the usual procedure where railway centres were established. History indicates that economical realisations in the industrial sense stand better chances of survival when they are backed up by progressive expansion. One-off exploits last for a relatively short time, and for March the end of an era came when the iron horse had reached the end of the road. The town in modern terms is a sandwich community in an area heavily influenced by Peterborough and King's Lynn - two places where industry is rapidly expanding. March is a town of character. Few towns the size of March possess a thoroughfare as impressively wide as Broad Street; at the planning stage it had been hoped to continue this street almost to the station and it is a pity it did not materialise. There is a trend to treat modern administrative buildings with panelling effect which does not always compare favourably with existing older buildings in rural communities. The contrast is too severe as can be envisaged at the Police Headquarters and the Crown Buildings. The embellishment and additions to the former High School for girls in County Road is not at all complimentary to the dignified facade of Fenland Hall, opposite.

The Gothic style is well in evidence at March. Four Anglican churches (one mediaeval) treated in this time-honoured tradition. Some nonconformist churches, too, were thoughtfully designed, especially St. Paul's Methodist Church based on psuedo-Gothic rendering in red brick, harmonising agreeably with brick-built residences nearby. The solid facade of Centenary Baptist Church set on a flight of steps adds dignity to an otherwise imposive effect upon the High Street. Three spires vie for prominence over the town: St. Wendreda's (c. 1380), St. Peter's and the elegant cemetery chapel in Station Road, which it is pleasing to add has not been pulled down; its presence enhances the vistas afforded by fine trees and bushes in this, the town's largest burial ground.

March is well covered by a mantel of trees seen to best effect from high vantage points. That is no fault, considering that the town has been compared to an oasis, there being in the reaches of fen an utter dearth of trees.

Perhaps Elwyn House portrays the town's finest aspect in Regency taste. High Street displays certain impressive Georgian facades, although March is really made up of a conglomeration of early and late Victorian residences with a fair sprinkling of Edwardian frontages. The riverside is made up of several interesting styles of architecture from the 17th century to modern times. It is there that planners have excelled. At one time it was the fashion in March to adorn porches with wrought-iron ornamental structures. A few remain, for example that at the entrance of the Wades Hotel. The craze for iron work seems to have inspired the Coronation Fountain in Broad Street (1911), an unusual over-adorned, top heavy monument with interesting sculptures depicting the Fens and March. It is unique, only one other, in Ireland, basically similar, cast at the same time.

What of the future? Can March face it with confidence or will it be with trepidation? The railway has been the town's life blood for just over 100 years. It has been an eventful century, a good innings really. When considering that the first metal was laid through March in 1846 purely as a through line, no-one imagined then that Whitemoor where swine fed on beechnuts and robbers hid, that it would one day be the home of 290 steam locomotives and the marshalling point of thousands of trains. The town's major employer was bound to decline sometime. That is the way of things, pinpointed as it is on the economical factor. The decline has taken place and it is fundamentally essential that March not only stabilise its population but plan to increase it. That can only be achieved by encouraging people to stay, and indeed, come to live in the town.

The controversial project embodied in the developing industrial and commercial site of Hostmoor must when everything else has been considered, be seen as a beneficial asset to the town - even if the development is forty years late. It will provide work for the town and the business effect is limitless and far-reaching. The fenreves of old had to give way and allow March to expand upon the commons. Hostmoor is the modern epitome of expressiveness and will to develop beyond the boundary of the town's architectural outline, similarly envisaged on a smaller scale at Longhill. It is simply history repeating itself. The development of more and more residential estates is no fluke either. The will to grow is undeniable and the siting of several new premises well away from the town centre speaks volumes for the town's future. That being the case it is essential to provide necessary facilities for the population in the future and to seize every opportunity that presents itself.

Another controversial issue, the establishing of a Category "B" prison on Whitemoor, while not desirably replacing the valued industrial presence of the marshalling yards, in effect will in the staffing of it bring a valued boost to the town's population. This can be measured in hundreds and that in turn must be of benefit to March traders. Thus as one door closes other doors open and a new era begins. After more than a thousand years on its island in the Fens, having witnessed the decline of the fisheries and river trade, the curtailment of wildfowling and demise of horse breeding, the railway almost gone . . . at the eleventh hour luck plays its hand. March receives a new, if different, lease of life in an era which history will underline as significantly cruel to larger communities.

Silent rails of Whitemoor